The Reminisc Activities
Training Manual

A Step by Step Guide • by Bernie Arigho

The Reminiscence Activities Training Manual

Published by
The Daily Sparkle
2 Town Hall Offices
North Street
Ashburton
Devon
TQ13 7QQ
Tel. 01364 652729
email: info@dailysparkle.co.uk
www.dailysparkle.co.uk

ISBN-13: 978-1466334038

The Daily Sparkle is a trademark of Everyday Miracles Ltd

Copyright © Bernie Arigho 2011

All rights reserved. No part of this book may be stored in a retrieval system or reproduced in any form whatsoever without prior permission in writing from the author. This book is sold subject to the condition that it shall not, by way of trade or otherwise, be lent, re-sold, hired out or otherwise circulated without the publisher's prior permission in any form of binding or cover other than that in which it is published, and without a similar condition including this condition being imposed on the subsequent purchaser.

Acknowledgements:
Designed and typeset by Penny Drinkwater
Illustrations by Joelle Brindley

Disclaimer:
Information herein is based on the author's extensive experience and knowledge. No part of the contents should be used in any way that may be considered unsafe.

The Author

* Bernie Arigho first became interested in reminiscence work when he was a student psychiatric nurse in 1986. He went on to specialise in the nursing care of older people, and as senior charge nurse at Acton Hospital in 1990 he set up a system of primary care nursing and life history profiles for the older patients.

* As part of his Master's degree in Gerontology at King's College, London, he researched and wrote a dissertation on the effects of older patients' reminiscences on the nurses caring for them (results published in the Nursing Times). His interest has always been in demonstrating the mutual benefits of reminiscence activities, and establishing models of good practice based on experience of working in the field.

* He became Age Exchange's Reminiscence Coordinator in 1992, responsible for developing training courses in reminiscence work skills and delivering outreach reminiscence project services. In this role he coordinated and supervised over 300 reminiscence projects in care settings, and provided training for approximately 500 course participants per year. In 2006 he outlined the principles of good practice in reminiscence work in 'How To Help Reminiscing Go Well' (published by Age Exchange 2006). He has also taught the theory and practice of reminiscence work on many courses of further and higher education, including drama students at the Royal Holloway University of London and the East 15 Acting School at the University of Essex.

* From 2004 to 2009 he was co-Director of Age Exchange, devising and obtaining funding for their outreach reminiscence programmes from the Department of Health, the City Bridge Trust and the National Lottery. These programmes developed cultures of learning and creativity within care settings for older people, linking reminiscence with music, dance, theatre and the visual arts, and exploring the links between creativity and health in old age. He promoted this work through many published articles in journals, conference presentations and media interviews.

* Now he works as a freelance reminiscence training consultant and project manager, aiming to support organisations in the UK who want to include reminiscence activities as part of their service, and seeking to set up well-established UK models of good practice in other countries. His most recent projects include an arts and health conference presentation in Australia, and training and consultancy work in Singapore and Japan.

Foreword

Welcome to this comprehensive guide to running reminiscence activities. We will provide you with ideas and exercises to aid you and your care team in becoming more experienced and knowledgeable about working with groups and individuals using this stimulating and person-centred approach. You will find that whether you are organising reminiscence projects, running group sessions, or working with individuals, the same guidelines to good practice apply. It is a fascinating and rewarding area of work, both for those doing the reminiscing and for those helping them. I hope my enthusiasm for the work comes across to you, and that this guide helps you to bring reminiscence activities into the lives of the people for whom you provide care.

Bernie Arigho

Learning methods and outcomes

This guide is aimed primarily at carers and activity organisers in care homes, although it will also be of interest to anyone wanting to learn more about the aims and methods of reminiscence work. The aim is to give you a comprehensive framework with which to plan and deliver reminiscence activities, together with many practical ideas for activities to offer your clients. This will enable you to provide reminiscence activities in a safe and stimulating way. The main goal, shared with *The Daily Sparkle*, is that everyone in care homes who can benefit from taking part in such activities is given the opportunity to do so.

The guide consists of five sections, divided into 24 parts:

Section 1 · *Introduction to Reminiscence* defines reminiscence work and outlines principles of good practice.

Section 2 · *How to Run a Reminiscence Group* looks at how to plan, structure and facilitate reminiscence group sessions, with examples of activities that are appropriate for different stages of a group's development.

Section 3 · *Creative Activities* focuses on linking reminiscence with a variety of different creative activities, with many examples that have been proven to have worked well over the years.

Section 4 · *Reminiscence in Dementia Care* considers how reminiscence can be especially helpful for people who have dementia, with examples of sensory and non-verbal activities.

Section 5 brings the guide to a close with features on three special applications of reminiscence work – oral history, projects with ethnic minority elders and intergenerational projects.

Throughout the guide there will be descriptions of activities for you to practise, followed by exercises to help you reinforce your learning. You will need a notebook to use as your Reminiscence Workbook as you work your way through the activities and exercises in the guide. This is for recording and evaluating your progress, and is a vital part of the learning process. Following the activities and exercises, there is further background information provided, but it is important that you complete the exercises first, before reading this and adding it to what you have learned.

For those who wish to develop further their skills and knowledge, participation in reminiscence training courses run by skilled and knowledgeable trainers is also recommended, as well as participation in projects alongside experienced workers who are skilled in delivering reminiscence activities programmes.

> By the conclusion of the guide, and on successful completion of the activities and exercises, you will have achieved the following main learning aims:
>
> - knowledge of the key characteristics of reminiscence activities
> - awareness of the varied personal and social benefits that can be achieved by participants
> - understanding of the principles of good practice in reminiscence work
> - understanding of the role and responsibilities of the facilitator in reminiscence groups
> - knowledge of the stages of development of reminiscence groups
> - knowledge of a range of activities that can be offered to reminiscence groups
> - understanding of how reminiscence can be used to foster the creativity of participants
> - knowledge of a range of activities linking reminiscence with writing, visual arts, drama, music and different crafts

- understanding of reminiscence work as part of the person-centred approach to dementia care
- awareness of the ways in which reminiscence can help to maintain the personhood of the person who has dementia
- knowledge of a range of sensory and non-verbal reminiscence activities
- understanding of the ethical issues and practical requirements of recording people's memories
- understanding of the special considerations required when doing reminiscence work with ethnic minority elders
- understanding of the principles of good practice in intergenerational reminiscence work
- knowledge of a range of reminiscence activities that can be used to bring younger and older people together in mutually beneficial ways.

Contents

The Reminiscence Activities Training Manual
A Step by Step Guide in 24 Parts

SECTION 1 — Introduction to Reminiscence
Parts 1 – 5

- Part 1 — *Reminiscence Activities* — 9
- Part 2 — *The Benefits of Reminiscence* — 14
- Part 3 — *Good Practice in Reminiscence Work* — 19
- Part 4 — *Good Practice in Reminiscence Work (continued)* — 25
- Part 5 — *Good Practice in Reminiscence Work (concluded)* — 30

SECTION 2 — How to Run a Reminiscence Group
Parts 6 – 11

- Part 6 — *What is a Reminiscence Group?* — 36
- Part 7 — *Planning and Preparation for Reminiscence Groups* — 42
- Part 8 — *Reminiscence Group Session Structure* — 47
- Part 9 — *Activities During the Opening Stage* — 53
- Part 10 — *Activities During the Development Stage* — 59
- Part 11 — *Activities During the Closing Stage* — 66

SECTION 3 — Reminiscence and Creative Activities
Parts 12 – 17

- Part 12 — *Reminiscence and Creativity* — 71
- Part 13 — *Writing Activities* — 76
- Part 14 — *Visual Arts Activities* — 82
- Part 15 — *Music Activities* — 88
- Part 16 — *Drama Activities* — 94
- Part 17 — *Craft Activities* — 101

SECTION 4	Reminiscence in Dementia Care Parts 18 – 21	
• Part 18	The Person-Centred Approach to Dementia Care	106
• Part 19	How Reminiscence Can Help	111
• Part 20	Group Activities Focusing on the Senses	117
• Part 21	More Sensory Activities	123

SECTION 5	Special Applications of Reminiscence Work Parts 22 – 24	
• Part 22	Reminiscence and Oral History	128
• Part 23	Reminiscence Work with Ethnic Minority Elders	135
• Part 24	Intergenerational Reminiscence	141
• EXTRA	The Daily Sparkle Reminiscence Newspaper	148

SECTION 1 • INTRODUCTION TO REMINISCENCE • PARTS 1–5

PART 1 Reminiscence Activities

Introduction

- The provision of purposeful activities in care homes for older people is now accepted as a healthcare essential, with consequent improvements in health and well-being for the residents, and a sense of fulfilment gained from their involvement. This guide is about how to include enjoyable and rewarding reminiscence activities as part of your care home's activities programme.

- Reminiscence is particularly valuable because it can lead to so many different types of positive activities for people to take part in, as will be shown in the detailed descriptions of hundreds of different activities throughout this guide.

- These activities meet important personal and social needs, and also give opportunities for residents to make positive contributions to the welfare of others through the sharing of their memories.

- Some residents may be limited by disability and frailty from fully participating in some activities, but reminiscence can be tailored to their needs, utilising their assets, and providing activities that are inclusive, enabling and enriching.

Reminiscence

'Reminiscence' – The recollection of one's life experiences

> "Memory is a way of holding onto the things you love, the things you are, the things you never want to lose"
> The Wonder Years

In everyday life people call such recollections 'memories', although more correctly reminiscences are the combination of many memories in order to recall the varied details of an occasion in the past. When we reminisce we experience associated feelings and emotions, connected with the experience being recalled, the experience of life since, and present feelings about life. Our role as 'Reminiscence Workers' is to help people reminisce in ways that achieve positive outcomes for them.

Since the 1970s in the UK there has been growing awareness of the personal and social benefits of reminiscence, especially, but not exclusively, in care settings for older people. There have been many reports and research studies to show that reminiscence activities can be stimulating and engaging for participants, and that they can lead to increased social interaction and improved well being.

The opportunity to reminisce with others about important times of our lives is something that most of us enjoy and take for granted, but this vital need is often missing for many older people in care settings who have no one to prompt or show interest in their recollections.

What are reminiscence activities?

What type of activities are we inviting people to take part in?

A 'reminiscence activity' involves the prompting and recalling of memories and experiences from the past, and then the expression and sharing of the reminiscence (if the person wants to).

Reminiscence activities may take many different forms, related to our personal preferences and to opportunities presented in our environment. A reminiscence may consist of a few moments' private recollection on our own, or it may be a shared story from the past in a reminiscence group.

This guide focuses on our role as organisers of reminiscence activities, with advice on how we can provide the right opportunities for people to reminisce in ways that are beneficial for them. The guidance is based on over 25 years' experience of observing what people have found helpful in the process of reminiscence. For example, part of good practice is to give people choices about what to reminisce about, encouraging them to reminisce when they want to, and respecting also when they do not want to. Some people may wish to spend some time creating an arts product from their memories, whilst others may wish to share their memories briefly in a small, friendly group setting. The work of giving other people opportunities to reminisce is known as 'reminiscence work.'

'Reminiscence work' – the stimulation of activities that give people the opportunity to achieve positive outcomes from their reminiscences.

Exercises for your Reminiscence Workbook

- Reminiscences can be prompted through any of the senses – an image, a sound, touch, taste, smell or a movement. These are called memory triggers. What triggers have recently prompted memories for you?

- Reminiscences can be related to experiences from any time of our lives. We can start recalling from about 2–3 years old! Select and write down some memories from different times of your life.

- Reminiscences can be about any aspect of life experience, for example, work, play, home and travel. What are the underlying themes of the memories that you selected? What were the memories about?

- Reminiscences may be kept private or may be shared with others. It's important that privacy is respected. Consider some of your own selected memories. How much of these would you be willing to share with others?

- The process of reminiscing may create an effect of some kind for us, for example, a change of mood, a new way of thinking, an attitude to a relationship, an effect on the person we share it with, a sense of achievement of some goal or purpose. Write about the outcomes of some of your recent reminiscences.

- We can express a reminiscence through any form of creative expression, for example, conversation, public speeches, written memoirs, poetry, painting, sculpture, craftwork, music, mime, drama and dance, to name but a few. How would you like to best express your reminiscences?

Different types of reminiscence activities

There is great choice and variety available as to the social context in which reminiscences can be prompted and expressed. It can take place on a one-to-one basis, or it can happen in a planned and organised group session. The group can meet occasionally, as and when you can arrange it, or they can meet regularly to develop their memories. It can be an on-going open group, or it can be a select group that meets for a set number of sessions. Parts 6–11 of this guide will take you through the processes of planning and delivering reminiscence group sessions in ways that best help your clients to achieve positive outcomes from the experience.

There is also a tremendous variety of ways in which memories can be prompted and expressed. The multi-sensory approach to prompting memories is exemplified throughout this guide, and a host of ideas for different types of creative activities is provided for you to choose from. The more choices you have available, the more likely you will find the right activities for your clients.

An opening reminiscence activity

Pass the basket

✸ This is an example of how to get the message across about reminiscence activities. Take a basket – it's something familiar to most people, and we often use it (or something like it) at the start of reminiscence projects and on training days. Other useful objects are shopping bags, string bags or even simple paper bags.

You can practise this with friends, colleagues or a group of your residents. Introduce the object to the group as a conversation piece. There are two main questions about the object: what could you put in it, and what does it make you think of? Has any of the group used such a thing before? If not, maybe it makes them think of someone else who has. If there is no memory of such an object, then what could they imagine putting in it? What other uses might it have?

Not every reminiscence activity will produce memories for everyone; it simply provides the opportunity. Give an example of your own about the object before passing it round the group, and giving everyone a turn to hold it and say what they think. Let them know beforehand that if they cannot think of anything, then that is perfectly valid and they can pass it on; someone else in the group may say something that triggers an idea or memory for them, and you can go back to them.

It's a simple and relaxed start to a reminiscence project, and the aim is for the group members to fill the empty basket or bag with a mixture of memories and imaginative ideas. More importantly, it aims to bring the group together, and give them a better understanding of how reminiscence activities work.

Exercises for your Reminiscence Workbook

- Collect feedback from participants about what it felt like to do this activity. What was interesting or enjoyable about it? Was it difficult or uncomfortable in any way?
- Was the object a useful and stimulating talking point? If so, what was it about it that made it so, and what other objects might also be useful for this purpose?
- What kinds of contributions did the group members make? What objects did they think of to put in the basket / bag?
- What memories were the objects associated with? What topics and times of life did group members appear to be quite comfortable talking about?

At the end of Part 1 trainees are expected to have:

- understood the value of activities provision in care settings
- understood the need for opportunities to reminisce in care settings for older people
- learned how to define reminiscence and reminiscence work
- carried out an exercise exploring the main characteristics of reminiscence – triggers, themes, level of privacy, effects and forms of expression
- carried out and evaluated an opening reminiscence activity that introduces the aims and methods of reminiscence work to a group.

In Part 2

In Part 2 we will focus on the benefits that can be achieved by reminiscence activities. There will also be more ideas for opening activities.

PART 2 *The Benefits of Reminiscence*

The main aim of reminiscence work is to help participants achieve positive outcomes from their reminiscences, and for the reminiscence activities to be a positive experience in their lives. People reminisce in their own individual ways, and will also benefit in their own individual ways. Our role is to provide them with helpful and conducive circumstances in which to recall and select their memories, and then the right kind of opportunities for expressing and sharing them. What kinds of benefits are we working towards with your residents? How can we help reminiscence to be a positive experience in their lives? We will do some activities to generate some ideas about the potential benefits of reminiscence.

Opening activities

Looking at postcards, photographs or selected images

❋ This activity works well as an opener when starting reminiscence work with new groups of residents, but for the purposes of reflecting on the benefits of reminiscence do this first with a small group of friends or colleagues.

Put together a varied collection of about 30-40 images, and make a display of them on a suitably sized table. Try to get a good mixture of the many different types of images that represent the many different types of places and human interests. Postcards work very well, but if you haven't got many of these, you could also use photographs or pictures from magazines. The important point is to have variety in the final display, for example, different landscapes, the seaside, waterfalls, parks, animals, houses, buildings of interest, film posters, adverts, maps, paintings, works of art, famous people. Ask the group to have a good look at all the images on the table, and eventually pick one or two that have a special interest or appeal to them. There may be a memory associated with the image, or it may be something that they like or find interesting. For whatever reason, ask them to pick up the image and tell the group why they made that selection. Go round the group and give everyone a turn. NB: This activity uses only visual triggers, but there is still great variety in the different types of images used. Make sure that everyone is able to see and look at the images.

Exercises for your Reminiscence Workbook

- What did you find out about the people in the group from the information that they shared?

- What links were made between different members of the group? Did they share any places or interests in common?

- Ask the people in the group individually what was enjoyable about this exercise. What did they learn from it or get out of it?

One-to-one reminiscing

* This activity is mainly designed for staff development, although some of the reminiscence ideas may well be useful prompts in the course of a reminiscence session, once you know that a group member wants to reminisce on that theme.

Make a list with your group members of about ten different topics for them to reminisce about with a partner. They can be quite specific topics, but with lots of choice.

For example:
1. A place that they have enjoyed visiting
2. A favourite piece of music
3. Something pleasant they did quite recently (a nice walk, a good meal, an interesting TV programme, a night out)
4. An especially memorable and enjoyable occasion from any time of life
5. Their first paid job
6. An interesting journey
7. A respected school teacher
8. An achievement of some kind (a certificate, a prize, driving licence, a successful job interview)
9. A game that they enjoyed playing
10. Their favourite films or film stars.

The group members can add anything to the list that would help to make it more interesting for them. Ask them to go into pairs, and pick a topic to talk about to their partner, each partner taking turns to do so. About 2-3 minutes each should be enough, but may be too long for some. The emphasis is on positive experiences, because we are trying to explore positive outcomes and help group members find topics that they would feel comfortable about sharing. Nevertheless, there may be some feelings of sadness or loss associated with them. The key point is that participants choose which topic to talk about, and they are enabled to say what they want to say on the topic.

Exercises for your Reminiscence Workbook

- Ask the participants in what ways the one-to-one sharing was different from the group sharing. In what ways did it feel different to them? How did it affect the way that they were reminiscing?

- Ask them what they thought was being exchanged during the one-to-one reminiscing. What was being given and received by the reminiscer and listener? In what ways was it a mutual exchange?

- Ask them what the effects of the reminiscences were for those who were reminiscing and for those who were listening.

- Finally, have a ten-minute discussion with the group on the different ways in which memories are important to people. Make a list of the main points arising from the discussion.

The benefits of reminiscence

The aims and objectives of reminiscence work

> "God gave us memories that we might remember roses in November"
> JM Barrie

From your exercise work it will be clear that there are many different positive uses to which reminiscence can be put, and that these vary from person to person, depending on individual life history, personality and present circumstances. It is not so much one's age that determines how one reminisces, but more the stage of life one is going through, and one's relationship with the past. Below is a summary of the positive outcomes that have been observed during reminiscence projects and in reminiscence research studies. It is important to recognise that benefits in reminiscence are mutually shared between the people reminiscing and those seeking to help them reminisce.

- It connects the past with the present in people's lives, and so gives them a sense of background and personhood.
- It helps to find common ground and shared humanity between people, and so improves social and community relationships.
- It helps us to understand other people and see their point of view.
- It passes on heritage between generations, and informs our knowledge of social history.
- It is a gift we can all give and receive that helps to build mutually beneficial relationships.
- It gives people an opportunity to express different aspects of their individuality, and so reinforce and strengthen their sense of identity.
- It helps us to look back and reflect on life, and in so doing provides greater understanding to face challenges in the present, and plan for the future.
- It helps people to remember more, make positive contributions and function at their best.
- It can lead to a wide variety of other social, creative and educational activities, providing a sense of fulfilment and pleasure for participants.

Conclusion

Participants in reminiscence activities take different things from the experience. For some it may be mainly a social activity, for some it may be a form of creative expression, and for others it may be an opportunity to pass on knowledge and learning. Our role as reminiscence workers is to help participants achieve their own personal goals from taking part. This requires observation and collection of feedback throughout the reminiscence activities, to ensure that participants are benefiting from the experience.

By the end of Part 2 trainees are expected to have:

- carried out and evaluated an opening activity that explores the benefits of reminiscence
- carried out and evaluated an activity that explores the differences between one-to-one reminiscing and group reminiscing
- chaired and written up the notes from a group discussion about the benefits of reminiscence
- acquired a knowledge of the positive outcomes that can be achieved through reminiscence.

In Part 3

In the next part, we will begin to focus on aspects of good practice in reminiscence work – the skills, knowledge and attitudes that help reminiscence workers to provide beneficial reminiscence activities programmes.

PART 3 *Good Practice in Reminiscence Work*

Introduction

Parts 3, 4 and 5 of this guide highlight standards of good practice in reminiscence work: the knowledge, skills and attitudes that help reminiscence activities to go well for participants. Whatever kind of reminiscence activities you are planning, these guiding principles are fundamental.

* The exercises in this section can be carried out as activities with residents. However, whenever possible, practising and discussing the activities with your colleagues first will provide an understanding of good practice issues before attempting them with your residents.

Person-centred care

Reminiscence work is part of the person-centred approach to care.

* 'Person-Centred Care means listening to people to find out what is most important to them. Assumptions are not made. Care is holistic and centres on the whole person: who they are, their life before, and how they currently feel. The emphasis is on what they can do, rather than what they cannot do. It is about working with people – not doing to them.' (from the Age Exchange DVD 'Listen to What I'm Saying')

Reminiscence workers need to have an appreciation of the individuality and uniqueness of each person, and a desire to try to understand that person's perspective. As reminiscences are stimulated and shared, each person's unique life-historical background becomes more apparent.

Good communication

Active listening and open questioning

The reminiscence worker strives to be a helpful prompter and listener, ensuring that a suitable distraction-free space for people's shared memories is provided.

An open exploratory style of questioning is more effective than a closed inquisitorial style. Closed questions are valid for obtaining basic information, but people need the opportunity to enlarge upon this should they want to. Open questions enable us to learn more about people as individuals. Leading questions, i.e.

those that put words into people's mouths, are not helpful in opening up their true thoughts and feelings. Examples of closed, open and leading questions are:

Closed question Did you like school?

Open question What did you like about school?

Leading question School was great fun, wasn't it?

Participants will be showing their feelings non-verbally as well as expressing them verbally, and we need to pick up on the cues that indicate their choices and preferences.

Genuine interest

When a participant has found something of interest that they want to share, the reminiscence worker becomes interested in return. Similarly, if the person does not want to reminisce about a certain subject, then the worker loses interest as well. The ability to show a genuine interest in, and appreciation of, the value of people's shared reminiscences springs from a recognition of them as gifts that are a privilege to receive.

Reminiscence workers need to show actively that they value people's contributions by demonstrating attentiveness and by giving back positive review during the closure of the session. There needs to be a primary respect for and interest in the contributor as a person in order for that person to be enabled to make their special contribution.

Respect for personal choice

Participants in reminiscence projects need to be able to make choices about all aspects of their participation. They should be respected and treated as valued volunteers on the project. They are volunteering their time and they are voluntarily sharing their personal memories. It is the reminiscence workers' responsibility to ensure that they are given a clear idea about what the project involves, so that they can make their own choices about participation. It may be that they would prefer a one-to-one format, or that at this time they would rather not take part at all.

Participants should be given choices about different ideas for activities and ways of sharing their memories. If participants are made aware of these different options, then they will feel more confident about taking part.

Activity

Mapping special places

This is another activity that is useful at the start of a new reminiscence project. It is a way of helping the participants and the reminiscence workers to get their bearings. Obtain a map of the UK and also a map of the world. If you know that many of the group come from the local area, then obtain a local map as well. Maps themselves are useful visual and verbal triggers, providing lots of information about place names and locations. The maps are linked with the theme of special places in our lives, for example, our hometown, where we were brought up, places that we moved to, places of education, places of work, places where we visited friends and relatives, day trips and outings or holiday resorts. Everybody gets the opportunity to name their special places, and the reminiscence workers mark each place with a coloured spot - a different colour for each person. Ask group members if they have any memories of those places that they would like to share. What is special about those places? What did they like or dislike about them? What happened there? What were the memorable characteristics of the place? Describe what it was like there. These memories can be added to the maps as captions on cards, attached to the spots by similarly coloured ribbons.

This activity sometimes lasts for 2-3 one-hour sessions, depending on how much group members want to share. Go round the group with each idea of a special place. Start with our hometown and where we were brought up, and then move on to the other types of places once everyone has had a chance.

Exercise *Evaluating the activity*

- Collect feedback from the participants as to their feelings about this activity. In what ways did they find it interesting and enjoyable, or not?
- Was the link between the theme of special places and working with the maps clear to the group members? Did mapping the special places assist group members to reminisce about them?
- Were all group members able to contribute something regarding special places in their lives? If not, what were the obstacles?
- What did you learn about the group members? What kinds of places did they want to reminisce about, and what kinds of memories were associated with them?
- Reflecting back on the benefits of reminiscence, what kinds of personal goals were individual group members achieving in this activity?

Fidelity and confidentiality

- By fidelity we mean 'faithfully reproducing and representing the experience that has been shared.' By confidentiality we mean 'only sharing with others what the person has given permission for you to share.'

> "It's not what you do, it's the way that you do it. That's what gets results"
> James Young/Sy Oliver

To be faithful to a shared story, one has to have properly heard and understood it, and so good communication skills, genuine interest and a good environment for communication are critical. If there is any misunderstanding or uncertainty on your part, then ask for clarification of the point. This is a way of showing the person that you value their story and you want to get it right.

When a high level of fidelity is achieved, as for example when a reminiscence worker accurately summarises what has been shared in a group activity, those group members recognise themselves as the authors of the memories shared, and feel that they have been individually listened to and valued.

With regard to confidentiality, explain to participants that one of the benefits of reminiscence work is to share information that has emerged from the reminiscence activities with care home staff, as for example in session reports, arts products or public displays of the work. If someone reveals a highly personal memory, make sure that they are willing for this to be shared. If someone shares something with you off the record and does not want anyone else to know, then this must be respected. The only exception to this is when there is reason to believe that the person is at risk of harm if this information is not shared. Discuss this issue with your care home manager, and ensure that your practice is in line with the care home's policy on confidentiality. Some of your residents may have someone to help them with these decisions, due to their inability to give informed consent.

Activity

What's in a name?

※ This is a staff development activity for you to practise with colleagues. It is intended to develop listening skills and to help you consider how we receive and summarise information.

Find a partner to work with and take turns to talk about your names. You can choose any part of your name to talk about, i.e. given name, second or third name, surname, married of maiden name, or nickname. You may talk about the origins of the name, the literal meaning of the name, different versions of your name held by different people, your feelings about your name, changes in your name at different times of life, or anything that comes to mind about your name. It is your partner's responsibility to learn what you want others to know about your name, and to tell them just that - nothing added and nothing taken away. Both partners will take turns to do this. After you have each heard the story about your partner's name, practise and rehearse what you have learned, making sure that you have got it right, and that you have your partner's permission to say what you are going to say. Then tell them the story of their name, and ask your partner for feedback on how well you did.

Exercise

Evaluating the activity

- What were the difficulties facing you in doing this activity?
- What skills were helpful in achieving a successful result?
- How did it feel to have someone else taking the responsibility for getting your name right?
- What kinds of memories were being triggered by thoughts about your name? What themes were they related to?

By the end of Part 3 trainees are expected to have:

✺ acquired an understanding of the principles of person centred care, good communication, genuine interest, respect for personal choice, fidelity and confidentiality in reminiscence work

✺ carried out and evaluated the 'Mapping special places' activity

✺ carried out and evaluated the 'What's in a name?' activity.

In Part 4

In the next part we will explore some other qualities of good reminiscence work, including the use of various multi-sensory memory triggers to give participants lots of choice about which memories to share.

PART 4 Good Practice in Reminiscence Work (continued)

Introduction

This part continues to outline some of the principles of good practice that help reminiscing to be a positive experience for participants.

Establishing trust and rapport

> "A strong safety net encourages healthy risk-taking"

There is an element of risk-taking for the participants when they choose to take part in new activities. Such risk-taking can be healthy and enjoyable, but it has to be based on a foundation of security and trust before they are able to fully engage. The opening phase is the key time for developing trust and understanding, and reassuring participants that their personal choices will be respected throughout. Typically, group members become more expressive and interactive as their confidence in the process and in the workers grows.

Some participants may express the fear that no one will be interested in their stories. You need to reassure them that everybody has interesting stories to tell about their lives. They also need to trust that you will remain true to all commitments and arrangements made regarding the activities programmes.

Respect and support for painful emotions

Reminiscence can generate a range of emotions, some painful and unpleasant, as well as joyful and pleasing. Sometimes there is a mixture of these feelings. Group participants are given the choice about which memories to share and which not to share, who to share them with, and how to share them. If they decide that a particular memory is too sensitive to share, then this is respected, and they are enabled to contribute in other ways.

When participants decide to share a difficult memory, reminiscence workers have a responsibility to ensure that painful feelings are properly listened to and supported with genuine empathy. Painful feelings about past losses, difficult circumstances and regrets are a part of everyone's experience of life, and it helps if these can be shared with others who are understanding and supportive. Some participants may share painful past experiences that they have come to terms with, and which they want to share now with others, because it is part of who they are.

The key point is about respecting people and putting them in control of their reminiscence project. We cannot change a bad experience in the past. Our responsibility is to ensure that the present experience is a good one.

Non-judgemental attitude

People come from different backgrounds, and will have experienced life in different ways. In every group there will be common links to be made, but also individual differences to be respected and appreciated. The past has not been the same experience for all of us, and we are all uniquely individual anyway.

Learning about the different perspectives of others helps to broaden our minds and develop a greater tolerance and respect for different attitudes. There may be disagreement about events and points of view, but there is room in the world for disagreement, respect and also a healthy working relationship at the same time. Reminiscence workers need to demonstrate an appreciation of the value of all reminiscence, and indeed every individual life. Diversity and unusual experiences should be as welcomed and faithfully represented as are commonly shared experiences and views. Group members get to know and appreciate each other better, because the focus is on the value of what each person is sharing from their lives.

Warmth

This describes a welcoming, approachable and positive person and space, thus creating an atmosphere of security, relaxation and mutual respect. As well as having a genuine enthusiasm and high regard for group members and their shared stories, reminiscence workers need to be able to remain good-humoured and to respond positively to the challenges and difficulties of trying to bring about worthwhile changes in care settings.

Many group members will appreciate a warm sense of humour in the face of life's absurdities, and enjoy an atmosphere in which it is easy to make others laugh and see the funny side of things.

Creative activities also lend themselves to the participants having fun while they are working together.

It is important to have the 'common touch' with participants, creating equal and mutual relationships with them. Sometimes, and especially in the openings to reminiscence sessions, it is helpful and much appreciated if the workers share a personal memory of their own to illustrate the process.

Use of memory triggers that stimulate the six senses

Memories are triggered through the six senses of vision, hearing, touch, taste, smell and muscle or movement memory. There is a wide variety of ways in which people can be helped to find and choose memories to share. A reminiscence worker's collection of memory triggers should include different types of images, sounds, textures, flavours, aromas and actions. When group members are new to the experience and uncertain about which memories to share, the non-verbal supplements to verbal triggers are a big help. When there are disabilities and communication difficulties, a much more non-verbal and wide-ranging approach is required. The multi-sensory approach helps to cater for everyone's needs. The objects will have different associations and memories for people depending on their life-experiences and their imaginations. There is no one right answer, and definitely no wrong answers.

It is important for participants to handle and use the objects as well as simply look at them. Movement and physical activity are very effective memory triggers.

Exercise *Making a list of memory triggers*

> This is something that you could do on your own, but it would be very helpful and productive to do it with a small group of colleagues (or friends) as this will generate a greater variety of responses.

> Memories are triggered through the six senses. Make a list of as many different specific triggers as possible under the headings provided. For example, music is a broad category and could be broken up into smaller headings, such as music from schooldays, songs liked by parents and grandparents, music on the radio, the first music that you liked and bought for yourself, concerts that you have been to, etc. Some objects will work in a combined way through different senses, making them very effective. A few examples are provided here to get you going.

Types of memory triggers

Visual · Postcards, magazines, colours...

Hearing · Sounds of steam trains, bells, music...

Touch · Fabrics, wooden objects, conkers...

Taste · Sweets, chocolate, mints...

Smell · Flowers, perfumes, herbs...

Actions and movement · Ironing, dancing, playing ball-games...

Keep adding to this list as more ideas are generated throughout your activities sessions. The list can also be the basis for creating your own collection of reminiscence objects and triggers. This is something in which you can involve everybody at the care home. Many of the best triggers are quite simple objects that are still commonly available in our communities, for example cotton reels, clothes pegs, old cameras. Try to start putting together a collection that stimulates memories though all the senses, and relates to different reminiscence themes. Many of these objects can also be found inexpensively in charity shops, car-boot sales and jumble sales.

Activity

What's my line?

This is a guessing game based on the famous old television programme, in which a panel had to guess the profession of the guest on the show.

In this version, group members are asked to remember a job they used to do, and do a mime of it for others to guess what it is. After the guessing is over, they can say more about their memories of this work if they want to. This works particularly well as a follow-up activity if the group has already been reminiscing and thinking about different types of work. It can be any kind of work, not necessarily paid employment, for example, a hobby or a type of housework. Some people may prefer to practise in pairs before demonstrating their mime to the whole group.

Exercise *Evaluating the activity*

- Obtain feedback from the participants about what this experience was like for them. Was it fun, interesting, difficult, helpful in triggering memories?
- What kinds of jobs and work did the group members mime?
- Did doing the mimes help them to recall more detailed memories? For example, did they remember more about the place of work and the people they worked with?

By the end of Part 4 trainees are expected to have:

* acquired an understanding of the principles of establishing trust and rapport, support for painful emotions, a non-judgemental attitude, warmth and the use of multi-sensory triggers in reminiscence work

* made a list of memory triggers that work through all the senses and that are related to a variety of reminiscence themes

* begun to create a reminiscence handling collection

* carried out and evaluated the 'What's my line?' activity.

In Part 5

Part 5 will complete the outline of good practice in reminiscence work, including the importance of working with broad reminiscence themes, and the value of offering participants a variety of creative opportunities.

PART 5 — Good Practice in Reminiscence Work (concluded)

Introduction

This part concludes the *Introduction to Reminiscence* section with some more principles of good practice in reminiscence work.

Use of inclusive and relevant themes

- A good reminiscence theme is one that includes the whole group. The opening of the project or session is concerned with getting to know the group and identifying their themes with them. No decision about which themes to focus on should be made without evidence that the group members are interested.

At first, the topic needs to be one of broad human interest, giving people lots of opportunities to contribute, and enabling them to choose from different times in their lives. There are a number of universal themes that are of general interest to people of all ages and cultures. For example, Food and Drink, House and Home, Work, Play, Entertainment, Travel, Fashion, Health, Education, Special People, Special Occasions and Special Places. As the project develops, it may become apparent that a narrower theme may interest the whole group. Examples of narrower themes include: Cooking, Housework, First Job, Childhood Games, Dancing, Schooldays, Seaside Holidays, Dressmaking, Bringing Up Baby, Love and Friendship, Weddings and My Home Town. When the chosen subject for a session is too narrow, it needs to be expanded to a broader topic.

Activity *Exploring a reminiscence theme (Entertainment)*

> "In reminiscence work there are no wrong answers"

This is a simple way of collecting a lot of ideas quickly from a group, and opening up a reminiscence theme so that group members learn that there were more choices around this theme than they realised.

Take a big, broad theme such as Entertainment. It is something that everybody is interested in, irrespective of age or cultural background, and it may take many forms. That makes it a good reminiscence theme.

Make a list with your group of as many different forms of entertainment as they can think of in 15 minutes. Write up their contributions on a flip chart or on something that everyone can see clearly. As group members start making suggestions, so these will trigger other ideas, and it helps to see them written up in a large format.

It may help to stimulate ideas if you offer the group a few broad types of entertainment, starting with home entertainment and going out for a night out, then moving to more specific activities such as sing-alongs around the piano and going to the cinema.

As with all reminiscence work, the beauty is that there are no wrong answers, only right answers. Entertainment is whatever individuals define it as for themselves. For some it might involve going to the opera house, and for others watching EastEnders on television. The more diverse your final list of entertainments is, the better and more representative it will be.

Exercise   *Evaluating the activity*

- Write up the group list of entertainment activities for your records as a future reference and resource. Discuss with the group if there are any activities listed that they would like to include in future group activities.

- Was this a theme that appeared to be of sufficient interest to the group to run a whole session on it? Did they have lots of memories associated with this theme that would need more time to share fully? What were these interests and memories?

- Discuss with the group if there are any activities listed that they would like to include in future group activities, if practicable.

A range of imaginative and creative opportunities

There are many different ways to express a memory or tell a story. People come to a reminiscence project with their own skills, talents and preferred ideas for activities. They may want to return to a creative activity that they have not practised for a time or to try a new creative activity. And, once group members have found stories that they want to share, they may want to take this a stage further. You will find certain memories lend themselves to particular types of creative expression, and without ideas and options about how to proceed, people may not be able to take this step forward. Parts 12–17 of this guide will focus on how to link reminiscence with creative activities.

Creative ideas cannot be imposed on group members. They can only be offered in response to individual and group development. Creative elements may hinder communication and group building if they are brought in too early for the group. We also have to be careful about the language we use in giving people options for activities. Terms such as 'art form', 'visual arts' or 'drama' may be off-putting for people who have never used this kind of language to describe what they liked doing, but have talked rather of drawing, painting or entertaining.

Activity   **Drawing a special place**

❋ This is an example of linking a form of creativity with reminiscence. In this case it is making a sketch drawing of a visual memory of a special place.

Explore and expand on the idea of 'special places' with the group. What is a special place? Make a list with them of all the different types of special places that they can think of, for example, somewhere one has lived, a particular part of a house, somewhere one has been to on an outing or day-trip, a holiday resort, a haven of rest, a lively night out, a concert hall, a restaurant, a church, or an historic building. Try to open it up to include as many different places of interest as possible, so that group members can make their choice.

Ask them to select a special place that they or a partner could do a simple sketch drawing of, based on the details and features of the place that they can recall. Some would prefer to draw their own special place, and others would rather someone else did it for them. It makes a good co-operative activity for one to describe their special place, and for another to listen and do a drawing of it. It is not so important to do a realistic drawing but rather to get the details of the memory right. There is no need to draw a perfect bicycle or horse, but simply to make it clear that there is a bicycle or a horse in this remembered place.

After the description of the place is complete, ask the person whose memory it is to think of a title for the sketch drawing. If the drawing was done for them, it is given back to them as being their shared memory. Give the person the opportunity then to tell the group the story of their special place, using the drawing as a guide to their storytelling.

Exercise — *Evaluating the activity*

- Make a note of the different special places that group members were recalling, and what was special for them about these places.

- Ask the group for feedback on this activity. What was enjoyable or interesting about it? What difficulties were involved in doing it?

- What did it feel like to recall and have drawn for them their memories of these special places?

- What evidence was there that adding the drawing to the remembering was helpful and conducive to further detailed reminiscence?

Good group facilitation skills, respecting equal opportunities

Careful preparation, good co-working, clarity about roles and flexibility about methods are essential to the delivery of a good reminiscence group. Everybody has interesting stories to tell about their lives, and everyone deserves the opportunity to do so.

Sometimes, visual and hearing impairment or degrees of dementia may combine with a general anxiety and lack of confidence that make it hard for group members to listen and be listened to. Using inclusive multi-sensory approaches and creative activities, and providing special attention for those who need it, reminiscence workers can help everyone to focus on what is happening, what they are doing and what the others are contributing. Issues around group facilitation will be explored in Parts 6 – 11 on How to Run a Reminiscence Group.

Monitoring and evaluation at every stage

There is a wide range of potential benefits that can be achieved through participation in projects such as these. The closures of sessions are a vital time to involve group members actively in evaluating the session that has just taken place and planning the next one. That way, the reminiscence workers are not relying entirely on their observations, and can concentrate on specific group and individual needs. Post-session evaluation meetings are also very important for gaining information on how the group is affecting individual group members, and how they appear to be benefiting.

Involvement of family and friends

The reminiscence activities are planned as special social events taking place for the residents alongside any other social events that they may enjoy with family or friends who visit and take them out. As with all aspects of care provision family and friends will want to know what their loved one is taking part in and how they are benefiting. They can be informed of the types of activities that are involved in, their level of participation and the general nature of the memories that they are sharing. There will also need to be communication about timings and dates, so that as far as possible the reminiscence activities do not overlap with visits or outings with family and friends.

With those of your residents who are cognitively impaired to such an extent that they cannot give informed consent, then family and friends have a vital role to play in assisting with reminiscence activities. They can provide background information about the person's life, especially knowledge about their hobbies and interests, their favourite pastimes and subjects of conversation, and their preferred types of activities. If the person has shared fragments of memories during an activity, then we can go back to family and friends to try to fill in some of the missing gaps. If a distressing memory is recurring frequently for the person, then ways of addressing this can be discussed. A new way of engaging well with the person may emerge from the work, and this can be shared with family and friends, some of whom may be interested in finding out more about how to use reminiscence.

Support, advice and guidance for workers in care settings

Our aim is not just to run a successful reminiscence programme for group members, but also to make reminiscence activities an integral part of care and life in general for care home residents. Management and staff in the setting need to know and appreciate how the reminiscence activities fit into the home's overall purpose and philosophy of care. There needs to be a widespread understanding within the home of the aims and methods of the work, and a respect for the project's need for time, resources and a suitable space to work in.

Where staff have been supported and encouraged to participate in these projects, care settings have become 'reminiscence venues', with all staff receiving information about the valuable reminiscence work happening there.

By the end of Part 5 trainees are expected to have:

* acquired an understanding of the principles of using inclusive and relevant themes, providing a range of creative opportunities, good group facilitation, monitoring and evaluation, involvement of family and friends and support and guidance for fellow care staff in reminiscence work
* carried out and evaluated an activity exploring the reminiscence theme of entertainment
* carried out and evaluated the 'Drawing a special place' activity.

In Part 6

We will start to look at the skills involved in running reminiscence groups, beginning with the role of the group facilitator and the stages of group development.

Section 2 • How to Run a Reminiscence Group • Parts 6 – 11

Part 6 — What is a Reminiscence Group?

Introduction

✸ This section of the guide (Parts 6-11) is concerned with how to set up and run reminiscence groups in care homes – group sessions where residents are given the opportunity to share their memories and achieve positive outcomes. There is a variety of ways of organising and running such groups, depending on the amount of time and resources you can put into the work and also on what works best for your residents.

We will be focusing on the idea of a reminiscence group as a closed group that meets regularly for a fixed number of sessions – an arrangement known as a reminiscence project. Under these conditions a reminiscence group can develop trust and confidence through a developing group process, work together to produce something based on their shared memories, and work towards bringing the project and the group to a satisfactory ending. Such a project requires refined organisational skills and can achieve a high level of group benefits. For that reason, it receives special attention in this section.

One-off sessions, single activities and open groups with no fixed number of meetings will need to be properly prepared and planned for as well, and can also be rewarding and enjoyable group experiences for your residents. The group members will not go through all the stages of group development that the project model provides, but there will still be opportunities to develop themes and do creative activities together. This section of the guide contains guidance on how to plan, deliver and evaluate group reminiscence activities, however you decide to organise and run them.

Activity — Shopping bag and special treat

✸ This is another simple and effective opening activity to get the message across about what reminiscence groups and activities are like, and to get a sense of whether or not it is something people would like to do. The aim is to create a relaxed yet stimulating environment for group members, some of whom may be quite new to this kind of group activity.

Find an interesting and eye-catching type of shopping bag. It could be made of canvas, leather or cotton string, or it could be a branded shopping bag from one of the big department stores. Introduce the activity by talking about the idea of going out shopping to buy yourself something that, for you, is a special treat. Talk about lots of different types of special treats to expand the topic. Then refer to different treats at different times of life – sweets, books, clothes, records, day trips. Extend it still further to include treats that other people have organised for you – birthday presents, other special occasions, surprise gifts. It could also be something that you would really like for yourself now, or anything at all that it would be nice to have. Somebody in a group once said 'world peace'!

Explain to the group that you will pass the shopping bag around them, and give everyone a chance to hold it and pretend to pull out the special treats that they have thought of. Reassure group members that they can pass the bag on if nothing in particular comes to mind, and that someone else in the group may trigger something for them. Start the activity yourself with a couple of your own examples, before passing the shopping bag around the group.

Exercise *Evaluating the activity*

- Ask the group for feedback about this activity. What kind of a group activity did it feel like?
- Discuss with the group if the atmosphere during the activity felt relaxed, informal, gentle, non-intrusive, friendly, warm, sociable,

> easy-going, interesting, and good-humoured. If not, why was that, and what could be done to improve the atmosphere?
>
> - What kinds of interesting and enjoyable topics emerged for the group members?
>
> - Give examples of how the group members shared memories and personal information, and so began to get know each other.
>
> - Discuss with the group members if they think it would it be useful for the group to have more reminiscence sessions together, and if so why and how many. What reminiscence themes might they focus on?

The four stages of a reminiscence group project

When considering how to run a reminiscence group project, there are four clear stages involved in the process. Each stage is vital to the success of the project, and each one requires its own set of tasks and objectives.

The planning and preparation stage

This is the critical stage that will determine whether or not you are adequately prepared, informed and resourced to provide reminiscence activities for a suitable group of residents. Many reminiscence groups flounder because this stage is passed over. Part 7 will focus on the planning and preparation work that needs to be done.

The opening stage

This marks the beginning of reminiscence group activities. It comprises the first two or three meetings when the group is coming together, and you are identifying with the members their preferred interests and activities regarding reminiscence. Part 9 will focus on group activities and group management skills that are helpful at this stage.

The development stage

This is the middle part of the project, when group members have developed greater confidence in the group and trust with the process, and when there is a clearer idea of the kind of reminiscence activities that the group would like to do. Part 10 will explore ideas for different types of reminiscence topics and reminiscence activities that are useful at this stage.

The closing stage

This is the final stage, when the group needs to complete its work satisfactorily, reflect on the positive outcomes that have been achieved, and move on to new projects and activities. Every project should have its ending in mind from the beginning, so that it is adequately prepared for and a satisfying sense of completion is arrived at. Part 11 will focus on the kinds of group activities that help to meet the needs of this final stage of the reminiscence group.

Different types of reminiscence groups

Every reminiscence group is unique. There is an infinite amount of variety possible in the way that groups will develop in their choices of memories to share, themes to focus on, and activities to participate in. Some groups may appreciate a sociable process of sharing memories, like a teatime or coffee morning chat. Some may prefer discussion groups interested in social history. Some may want to be more engaged in games or physical exercises. Some may want to focus on a creative activity, such as artwork or needlework, whilst they intermittently share memories. Some may want to produce something based on their memories, such as a booklet, a collage or a little piece of theatre. Our role is to find the right kind of reminiscence activity for the group.

Activity — *What is the point of a reminiscence group?*

This is a question I was quite reasonably once asked at the start of a reminiscence group by someone who wanted to talk to me about some of his memories, but who did not want to sit and listen to other people sharing *their* memories.

Having done a group-reminiscence activity with a group of friends or colleagues, ask them to have a ten-minute discussion on the reasons for inviting people to take part in a reminiscence group. What can be achieved in a reminiscence group, and how can group members benefit?

Exercise — *Listing the benefits of reminiscence groups*

- Make a list of the main points arising from this discussion. What can a group offer that one-to-one reminiscing cannot? What are the potential advantages for the participants of taking part in a reminiscence group?

The benefits of group reminiscence

> "No man is an island entire of itself"
> John Donne

From your exercise work it will be clear that there are many different positive outcomes that can arise from inviting your residents to take part in group reminiscence activities. Your residents are all individual people with different personalities and in different circumstances (other than all being residents in care homes) who will benefit in their own individual ways. Our aim is to run the right kind of group activities for all the residents to achieve something positive for them. The following list summarises the varied positive outcomes that have been reported and observed during evaluation of reminiscence groups in care homes. Once again, it is important to include the benefits to activities organisers and care staff of being involved in such groups.

* Increased social interaction and improved social relationships within the care home
* Increased self-esteem, sense of identity and self-worth for the group members through participating and sharing their memories positively
* The pleasure and satisfaction of creativity within the group
* Involvement of the wider community in the project through publicising the group activities
* Development of person-centred care skills for care home staff
* Group members learning from each other's experiences, knowledge and insights
* Development of group identity and a sense of belonging to a new group
* Promotion of positive role models of older people in care homes

The importance of co-working

Before we begin to examine in detail the various tasks involved in organising and running reminiscence groups in care homes, it is a good time to emphasise the importance of having a co-worker in the group with you. This should be someone who shares your interest and enthusiasm for activities provision, and someone who can assist you with the responsibilities of group facilitation. This is to ensure that the group is adequately planned for and resourced, and that group members are adequately supported and monitored throughout the whole process.

By the end of Part 6 trainees are expected to have:

✸ carried out and evaluated an opening group activity that aims to introduce a group to the aims and methods of reminiscence work

✸ acquired an understanding of the four stages in the life of a group

✸ chaired and made notes from a group discussion on the value of sharing memories in groups

✸ acquired an understanding of the benefits of group reminiscence

✸ appreciated the importance of co-working.

In Part 7

In the next part we will look at how to plan and structure reminiscence group sessions, and how to run a series of group sessions with a selected group of residents. I will describe an 8-session model, as this has proved to be a practical and successful format in many hundreds of care homes.

PART 7   *Planning and Preparation for Reminiscence Groups*

Different project models

There are choices to be made about how many sessions you are going to run with your reminiscence group, and how frequent they are going to be. There is also a choice to be made about whether the group is closed for its duration or open to all-comers. These choices depend on the time and resources available to run the project, the preferences and needs of the residents and your specific aims and objectives for the work. However you decide to organise the group activities, the guiding principles of planning, delivery and evaluation will be the same. The 8-session project model has been successfully used by Age Exchange for 25 years, and is a useful example of good practice.

The 8-session model

This model has proved workable, and capable of achieving the aims of creating a new reminiscence group and developing enjoyable group activities for the residents. There has to be complete understanding with the responsible manager within the care setting about all the factors that will ensure that the reminiscence group can succeed, for example, a regular meeting time, a suitable space for the meeting, and regular participation by two named workers who meet before and after each session for planning and evaluation.

Eight reminiscence group sessions, held weekly, are timetabled for a group of about six to eight older people in the care setting. If there are more people who would like to take part, then they can take part in the next group project that you run.

The project has three phases of growth. The first two reminiscence sessions form the opening to the project, with the emphasis on introductions and the creation of a warm and supportive atmosphere in the group. These initial two sessions lead to the identifying of reminiscence themes and preferences about activities. The next four sessions build on the first two by focusing on particular themes, and include the option of a creative activity. The final two sessions bring the reminiscence group to a close, reviewing the whole project, appreciating and celebrating the work done by the group, and considering ideas for future activities.

The Opening

Session One Opening session

Introductions

Opening general activities

Finding themes and activities of interest

Session Two More opening general activities to find themes and activities of interest

Development

Session Three Developing more specific themes and activities

Session Four Developing more specific themes and activities

Session Five Developing themes and activities

Session Six Developing themes and activities

Closure

Session Seven Developing themes and activities

Working towards completing the activities

Session Eight Bringing the group to a close

Review of the group's achievements

Ideas for other activities in the future

Variations on the 8-session model

There are many ways in which the above model can be tailored to meet local specific needs. Eight sessions may not be enough for your group, and it may be decided that 10 or 12 are required for the group to achieve everything it planned.

There is also the possibility that in the closing stage the group decides that it wants to continue indefinitely, in which case the closure of the group is postponed and the development continues. Some groups have found that a week is too long between sessions and that they need to be run more frequently – say, two or three times a week, or even on a daily basis.

Factors to consider before starting

> "To be prepared is half the victory"
> Cervantes

❋ Whatever the project model that you employ, there is a number of factors that you need to consider before planning the opening group session.

Staffing

You, and a colleague who is interested in running reminiscence activities, will staff the project. The time spent on working on this project must be valued as integral to the overall aims and work of the care home, and all assistance given to the co-workers to commit to it.

Dates and day of week of reminiscence sessions

You will need to discuss with all concerned the most convenient day of the week for the group to meet, and then make sure that these dates are in everybody's diaries.

Suitable room for the group session

Ideally you want an accessible and comfortable room that can accommodate the group, and most importantly be free from any interruptions or distractions for the duration of the session. This needs to be guaranteed, and everyone in the care home aware of it.

Timings

You are looking for a ninety-minute slot, allowing about fifteen minutes for the planning meeting, sixty minutes for the reminiscence session and fifteen minutes for the evaluation meeting. The tea break can come at the end of the session, or it can be incorporated as part of the session, but it should not come as an unplanned interruption.

Group selection and size of group

Choose to invite those residents whom you believe would benefit from a group such as this, and who would enjoy the opportunity to share memories. If communication difficulties are severe within the group, you may need to keep the numbers down to 4-6 residents.

Aims for the project

In addition to considering the general benefits of reminiscence, write up a list of individualised aims for the group members. Discuss these with colleagues, and involve group members in setting their own personal objectives for the group.

Exercise — *Making a proposal for starting a reminiscence group*

Write a proposal for starting a reminiscence group project in your care home, using the following headings:

- Aims and objectives (how these meet the care home's mission)
- Number of sessions
- Staff involvement
- Group selection
- Room choice
- Day of week and dates
- Timings.

Inviting people to take part

After you have talked to group members about the project, and shown them some examples of reminiscence activities, you can give each one an invitation card that lets them know that their attendance is requested and that their participation would be appreciated. The invitation card helps to set the right sociable and friendly tone for the group, and acts as a reminder for the guest to take part - something to put in their diary.

This is an example of the kind of information and wording that the invitation card can include:

Dear (group member),

You are invited to join a group that will give you the chance to share your memories in a friendly, easy-going way.

The group meetings will continue (day of week, date and time) and then will take place every week at the same time for the following 7 weeks.

(Your name) and (your co-worker's name) will be there to support the group with lots of activities for you to choose from.

We look forward to sharing an enjoyable and interesting time with you.

Exercise — **Creating an invitation card**

- Design an invitation card for prospective members of the reminiscence group.
- Use language that is friendly and sociable, including information about what kind of group it is, and the timings involved. Make the card attractive and convivial, not formal and businesslike.

By the end of Part 7 trainees are expected to have:

- acquired an understanding of the organisation and purposes of the 8-session model of reminiscence project, with an appreciation of its possible variations
- acquired an understanding of all the factors needing to be considered before commencing the work
- written a proposal for starting a reminiscence group in a care home
- written and designed an invitation card for prospective members of the reminiscence group.

In Part 8

Next time we will focus on how to structure each session, so that it is properly introduced and concluded, and group members have time to share their memories. In this way, the group stands out as a special occasion for all concerned, and also becomes integrated into the rest of life in the care home.

PART 8 Reminiscence Group Session Structure

Session structure

This part focuses on how to structure each session, so that it is properly introduced, developed and concluded. In this way the group session can be an enjoyable and memorable social occasion in its own right, as well as becoming integrated into the overall pattern of life in the care home.

Each session has a distinct 3-part structure – beginning, middle and end – with a planning meeting beforehand and an evaluation meeting afterwards.

Timings

These are the suggested timings that help to ensure that there is a good structure to the session, and that all objectives will be achieved:

Pre-session meeting – 15 minutes
Opening to session – 10 minutes
Middle session – 40 minutes
Closure of session – 10 minutes
Post-session meeting – 15 minutes.

You will need time before the pre-session meeting to set up the room for the group. You will also need some time between your pre-session meeting and the opening to the session to help residents to come to the group. An hour is allotted to the reminiscence session, although with some groups it may feel a little too long or not long enough. This is something you have to adjust as the project progresses, allowing leeway either side.

Pre-session planning meeting

You can have this meeting with your co-worker after you have set up the room for the group, and before the group members come into the room. This is the time to run through the session plan together so that you are both clear about what you want to do. What are the main theme and sub-themes for the session? What reminiscence prompts and triggers will be used in the session? What equipment is needed, and is it in good working order? How will the session start, develop and finish? What are the main activities that you have planned? How have you arranged the seating so as to ensure that communication in the group is facilitated? This means ensuring that the two co-workers are placed next to group members who need most support and assistance.

The key task of this meeting is to ensure that the co-workers are aware of their roles and responsibilities at every stage of the group session. As one co-worker takes responsibility for introducing an activity, the other is responsible for monitoring and assisting group members.

Beginning of session

The opening of the session is a time for welcomes and introductions, setting the warm, friendly and respectful tone for the group. At the start of the project some time needs to be spent on repeating the aims and methods of the group. Emphasise to the members that this is their group and their opportunity to decide what they want to do. Less time will need to be spent on basic introductions to the project as the project progresses.

During the opening of the group there is the opportunity for a short activity that brings the members together and provides a stimulus for the rest of the session. Introductions by name is itself an activity, requiring planning to ensure that it is done in the most helpful, enjoyable and interesting way for the group members. Activities such as passing round an interesting object (like the basket or shopping bag) are good ways to bring the group together. As the members identify their interests and preferred activities, the opening to the session can become more tailored to the group.

Middle of the session

This is the main part of the session, taking the majority of the time, and the part in which the group finds its reminiscence themes, preferred activities and interests, and takes part in activities that build on them. At the start of the project the main aim is to help the group find its preferred themes and activities. The rest of the project is concerned with working on these identified interests and bringing them to a satisfactory conclusion. NB: Parts 9, 10 and 11 of this guide list a wide range of reminiscence activities to choose from with your group, such as exploring and using reminiscence objects, talking in small groups, sharing with the whole group, listening to music, singing and dancing, and playing games.

Closure of session

It is most important that time is made for this part of the session, because it fulfils the tasks of reflection and reorientation for the group. A sudden end whilst in the stream of shared reminiscing is dissatisfying and leaves a sense of incompletion, all of which works against what you are trying to achieve. Leave enough time for finishing off what group members wanted to say, and for some review of what has happened in the group.

Ask for feedback from group members about the session, and thank them for their contributions by accurately repeating some of the memories they shared. Have a discussion about what the group might do next time, making suggestions based on what has come out of the session. In this way, the closure of each session forms a bridge to the next session, and the group members are involved in planning and decision-making about the group at every stage of the project. There may be time for a short group activity, building on what has happened in the group, such as singing a song, or making a list of favourite things. Finally, have a parting private word with everybody in the group to thank them for taking part, and to ask them once again if they have enjoyed the session.

Post-session evaluation meeting

The evaluation meeting with your co-worker is important for your own learning and development, and also for the development of your working relationship with your co-worker. Together, you can look back at the objectives for the group and the individual group members, and search for evidence of these objectives being achieved.

Make notes at this meeting, because this is the best time to recall what happened in the group. Did the session go according to plan? What worked well? What did not work well? How could it be improved? It is important to focus on individual group members and individual contributions, rather than simply making generalisations about the group. We have found it helpful to do a diagram of the group immediately afterwards, indicating where everybody sat in relation to each other, listing memories and contributions under each person's name, and drawing lines between people when there was a link or interaction between them.

Exercise — *Putting together a starter reminiscence collection*

> You are approaching the time when you are ready to start running a complete group reminiscence session, and it is essential that you have to hand a collection of multi-sensory reminiscence objects, as already outlined in Part 4. How is your collection coming along? Try to involve all the senses in reminiscence, and have objects related to a range of different themes. List all the objects you have, the senses through which they can trigger memories, and the different themes that they relate to.

Checklist and plan for opening session

Session One — **Checklist of memory triggers and equipment**

- Old shopping bag
- Collection of varied reminiscence objects
- Selection of audio-cassettes and CDs
- Tables and trays for display and sharing of memory triggers
- CD and cassette player

Session Plan — **Opening**

- Background music as group members enter
- Introduction to the project
- Today's themes: getting to know each other, finding out what memories we like to share and what activities we like to do
- Opening activity: What would you put in the shopping bag?
- Names

Middle

- Exploring the objects and selecting something of interest
- Small-group discussions about the objects selected
- Sharing with the whole group
- Large-group discussions on reminiscence themes

> **Closure**
> * Appreciation of contributions
> * Feedback on the session
> * Ideas for future themes and activities
> * Looking forward to the next session and the rest of the day

One-off reminiscence sessions

These can be enjoyable events, and are a good way of finding out if a group might be interested in taking part in an 8-session project, in which more could be achieved. It could be run on the lines of the opening session to a project, with no specific theme, aiming at giving people a taste of what a reminiscence session is like through a general introduction. Such a session may be particularly helpful in producing evidence to back up your belief that the reminiscence group will meet some of your residents' needs.

Exercise — *Introductory reminiscence session*

> You can do this with a small group of friends, colleagues or residents. The aim of this exercise is that you practise and become familiar with the process of opening, developing and closing a group reminiscence session.

> "A whole is that which has a beginning, a middle, and an end"
> Aristotle

Using the session already outlined, run a one-off introductory reminiscence session with a small group (for the purposes of this exercise, it can be smaller than normal - say 3 or 4 people). Make sure that you give adequate time to all the stages of the process, including the planning and evaluation meetings before and after the session, and the opening, middle and closure of the session itself.

Exercise — *Writing a session report*

> In the post-session evaluation meeting with your co-worker make a note of what actually happened in the session – the sequence and broad timings of activities that took place. This is not always the same as the session plan intended!

- Use the guidelines previously outlined (under post-session evaluation meeting) to discuss what happened in the group session.
- Focus on individuals – their contributions, assets and strengths – and specific examples of group bonding.
- Make some notes on the critical closing part of the session – the feedback you obtained from group members, ideas for future sessions, and any evidence that the aims and objectives are being achieved.
- Make a special note of your own personal and professional learning – aspects of your work that you would like to improve, evidence of the skills and resources that you have demonstrated, and areas of the work that you would like to develop.

Conclusion

In this part we have concentrated on the session structure, comprising the pre-session planning meeting, the beginning, middle and closure of the session, and the post-session evaluation meeting. This structure provides an effective framework for all your reminiscence activities sessions.

By the end of Part 8 trainees are expected to have:

- acquired an understanding of the overall structure of each reminiscence session, with an appreciation of related timings
- acquired an understanding of the tasks and responsibilities of each part of the session structure: the pre-session planning meeting, the opening to the session, the development of the session, the closure of the session, and the post-session evaluation meeting
- started to enlarge upon a reminiscence handling collection, making it more multi-sensory, multi-thematic and inclusive
- written a session plan for a one-off introductory reminiscence session
- run and evaluated a one-off introductory reminiscence session, having given adequate time to all the stages of the process.

In Part 9

In Part 9 we will look at some more ideas for group reminiscence activities that have worked well in the opening phase of a project.

PART 9 — Activities During the Opening Stage

> "When we seek to bring out the best in others, we somehow bring out the best in ourselves"
> William Arthur Ward

These kinds of activities help the group to identify their reminiscence themes and preferred activities. They do not focus on a specific theme, but rather offer a range of themes for group members to choose from, and focus on, in future sessions. The opening to the project consists of the first two sessions, although some groups may identify specific themes of interest to them in the first session, and begin developing these in the second session. We have already done some activities that are helpful early on in a project, such as Looking at Postcards and Mapping Special Places. Here are some more.

Take your pick

* This is a highly recommended way to start a reminiscence project. It enables the group to explore a range of reminiscence objects related to many different themes, and to have memories and thoughts stimulated through the six senses.

Make a display of the objects that is accessible to the group. This may be on a central table or it could be passed round the group on a tray. Group members get a chance to look at, touch and use the objects, and pick an object that is of interest or has a memory attached to it. It's a simple idea, but it emphasises respect for personal choice and individuality, with group members enabled to decide what they want to focus on.

I must have done this activity over a thousand times, and it has never been the same twice. The objects have an infinite variety of meanings and associations for people, and stimulate all sorts of interesting thoughts and connections.

The point of the activity is not to get the right answer - there is no right answer - but rather to utilise the power of the objects for stimulating memories and the faculty of imagination. Group members may also be reminded of things that are not in your display, but which would make excellent additions to your collection.

Some groups may find making a choice somewhat difficult or even unappealing, in which case the objects can be explored one by one with the whole group. You could put the unopened box of objects on a table in front of the group, and gradually unpack it and study the objects together, adding an element of mystery and surprise to the activity.

As with many of these activities, you may find that it helps group members to think and communicate better, if you and your co-worker divide the members into two smaller groups. Once everyone has had a chance to explore the objects and have their say, then you can come back together, and give people a chance to share their memories with the whole group.

Listening to a selection of reminiscence readings

This is a nice way to identify topics of interest to the group. Select a range of quotations from published sources related to the broad reminiscence themes of Food and Drink, House and Home, Work, Play, Entertainment, Travel, Fashion, Health, Education, Special People, Special Occasions and Special Places. Read them aloud to the group yourself, or identify someone from the group who has a good reading voice.

* Age Exchange provides excellent source material from the 1930s and 1940s. Age UK has a website devoted to reminiscence called 'The Time Capsule' with archives of memories from all the post-war decades, and *The Daily Sparkle* is a reminiscence newspaper and great resource for quotes, sayings and poetry. Use quotations that are evocative and clear in their meaning, so that group members can be prompted to share their related reminiscences. Experiences and views vary greatly depending on life-history and individual differences.

For example, on the subject of food:

* "We used to have the Hygienic Bakeries call every day with bread. As kids we all looked forward to Saturdays. This was the day that most of the cakes were on his van. The fresh cream puff pastry sandwich was the 'bees knees'."

This is an appetising introduction to food, and an invitation for the group to share their stories about shopping for bread, deliveries, and special treats. What was the 'bees knees' for them?

Looking at photographs together

This is a nice familiar activity that helps to ease a group into reminiscence. Make sure that everyone is able to see and look at the photographs. Obtain a wide selection of photographs that are full of visual information about subjects such as home, the neighbourhood, the streets, transport, friends, family, clothing, hobbies and interests, holidays, school and types of work. You can include some of your own photographs as well, as a way of inviting group members to bring their own photographs to future sessions. It is not a test of memory, but rather a relaxed social activity and an opportunity for conversation about group members' lives. Pass the photographs round the group, and wait for any comments and recognitions that group members have. It may help with communication to break the group up into two smaller groups, as with the 'Take your pick' activity.

Reminiscence slideshow

A variation on the above activity is to change the format and the viewing experience by obtaining slide images of the photographs and projecting them through a slide projector, or as computer generated images. This is a very different experience, maybe not quite as sociable and conducive to conversation, but helpful in focusing and concentrating on the photographs so that every detail is appreciated. Group members can comment as and when they see something that prompts them to want to share something. The slideshow format is in itself a reminiscence experience that may bring back memories of watching slides at home, at school or in a club.

Passing round a variety of fabrics

Make a collection of different kinds of fabrics and clothing materials for group members to touch and feel. These can be cut-outs from articles of clothing or rolls of material, or they can be the original article itself. For example: woollen gloves, nylon stockings, starched collars, lace, a silk scarf, and various types of material such as leather, satin, brocade, crepe, chiffon, fur. Another option is to sew different fabric squares onto an apron, and pass this round the group as a kind of reminiscence patchwork.

Encourage group members to touch and stroke the fabrics, and say what it feels like. The idea is to give choice and enable expression of preference. The emphasis is on enjoyment and making choices. The sensations coming through the sense of touch, combined with the colours and styles of the fabrics, may well also prompt some memories. Many of these textures may be very familiar to group members, and have associations with dressing up, going out, growing up, changing fashions, having children, and dressmaking.

Our songs

Early in the project we try to find out from the group members what kinds of music and songs they like. The songs people know and love can be related to every aspect of life. Once again the main reminiscence themes are a good place to start, for example, songs related to food, home, friendship, work, play, schooldays, entertainment, special occasions, special places and special people. Make a list on a flip-chart with the group as they name their favourite songs and music. Most popular songs are quite easy to obtain on CD now, and can be played back to the group at later sessions. They are a very useful way of providing a soundtrack for the beginning and ending of sessions, and of course the group members may well know the words and be able to sing them.

There may be an issue regarding the legality of playing copyrighted CDs and other recordings in care settings other than residential or nursing care homes. If you are uncertain, check this with your manager. There will be more on the use of music in reminiscence in Part 15.

Listening to a variety of sounds

This is another nice relaxing activity that focuses on a specific sense – in this case that of hearing. Once again you must make sure that this is an activity that everyone can participate in with assistance. The sense of hearing can be a rather neglected area in reminiscence work, with music being often the only prompt used, but there is so much more to it. The BBC Sound Effects Library is a wonderful resource with sixty CDs of sound effects and ambiences from around the world – the sounds of nature, birdsong, animals, babies, the sea, weather, industry, street sounds, transport, to name but a few.

Remember that smell

This activity focuses on objects that have a characteristic aroma, so you need to make sure that everyone in the group has a sense of smell and is therefore able to take part. Aromas can prompt positive feelings and emotional memories for people, such as relaxation, safety, love and security, as well as their polar opposites. People will tend to stay with, and return to, an aroma they like, and quickly remove themselves from one they do not. There may be memories and stories attached to the aromas, or they may give rise to more generally positive or negative feeling. There will be no one aroma that is right for everyone, or that means precisely the same thing to everyone.

Pass a variety of objects around the group that have different aromas related to different aspects of life – work, the home, food and drink, fashion, important people, travel, the natural world, entertainment, health care and hygiene. You can use a variety of foods, flowers, herbs, fabrics and clothing, perfumes, soaps, cleaning and polishing materials. It's important not to recreate a test situation that puts people under pressure and creates a sense of failure. It is simply an opportunity to share any memories and feelings that may arise.

What is your idea of a good night out or a good night in?

There will be a wide range of ideas regarding how to spend an enjoyable night, varying from person to person. Open up the topic for the group, pointing out all the different types of activities that it could involve, including just having a quiet restful night in. It may be that some people believe that they had very little spare time for leisure activities, and that these were relatively few and far between, making them all the more special.

What shall we buy with these coins?

Open up an old purse containing pre-decimal money with the group. Count out and add up the money together and work out with them what would have been the best way to spend this money during a particular decade, for example, the 1950s or 1960s. All the choices available should be considered before the final decision is made. You can make a shopping list with the group.

Exercise *The opening activity*

After you have run one of these activities, evaluate it and write a report according to the guidelines in Part 8. In addition to these general guidelines for evaluation, reply to the following specific questions.

- What reminiscence themes emerged from the activity as being of general interest to the group?
- Were there any specific reminiscence themes that some group members wanted to avoid, such as schooldays, parents, Christmas or holidays?
- Which triggers worked particularly well with individual group members?
- What kinds of creative activities were the group interested in? For example, playing games, singing, drawing, writing or craft activities? Could some of these involve the whole group?
- Would it be helpful to do some more general activities with the group, before focusing on a specific theme?

By the end of Part 9 trainees are expected to have:

- carried out and evaluated a selection of opening activities that help a group to identity their reminiscence themes and preferred activities.

In Part 10

In Part 10 we will focus on activities that may be helpful for the group during the development stage of the project, once their preferred themes and activities have been identified.

PART 10 Activities During the Development Stage

> "Never underestimate what people can do"

By this stage the group has hopefully become more familiar with the process of sharing memories, and understanding and confidence in the group is increasing. Group members will have identified some themes of special interest and indicated the kinds of activities they like. The following activities have been used successfully with groups after we had established with them that it was something that they wanted to try. These activities often follow on naturally from what has come out of previous sessions.

In deciding what activities to offer your group, don't underestimate what they may enjoy doing and remember not to impose an activity on them because you think it's a good idea, without there being clear signs from them that it is something they would like to do.

There will be lots more ideas for development activities in Parts 13-17 on creative activities.

Exploring a theme

For example, Games and Play

* This is a simple listing activity that enables you to explore a theme in depth with a group, and helps to include all the group members by making sure that the subject is fully covered in all its aspects.

It helps to have a few related objects for group members to handle before making the list, so that attention is focused on the theme, for example, a skipping rope, some marbles, a conker and a ball. Use a flip-chart to write up all the different games that group members can remember playing in their lives - not only in childhood, but all through their lives. This is an effective way of generating lots of ideas quickly. Make sure that as many different aspects of the subject as possible are included, for example, family games, children's games, street games, playground games, party games, holiday games, team games, board games, pub games, toys and puzzles, to mention just a few. Following this activity, you will have more ideas for objects for your reminiscence collection, and you can begin to create 'handling' collections related to specific reminiscence themes.

Reminiscing on a theme

For example, Entertainment

When you have obtained enough objects related to a specific theme, you can run an activity using those objects to focus on the theme. Group members get the chance to have multi-sensory triggers to help them remember more about the subject, and to have time to share their thoughts and memories in group discussions. For example, for groups that have enjoyed the subject of entertainment (both at home and going out), this activity will open it up further and help them to enlarge on what they have already shared.

Objects related to this subject might include records, songbooks, playing cards, board games, music scores, film posters, pictures of film stars and cinemas, dance band music, theatre programmes, copies of the Radio Times and TV Times, lantern slides, theatre magazines and Picture Post magazines.

Bring a thing

* The idea is that the residents are invited to bring their special things to the group, show them, and tell the members the stories behind the objects, and why these things are important to them.

  This is a follow-on from the 'Take your pick', and 'Looking at photographs'. It may take some time for group members to consider this idea. They may need to search through their possessions before they find something suitable. Some items may be considered too precious and intimate for the group. All personal photographs and personal items are very precious personal possessions, and it should be regarded as a great privilege if members decide to show these to the group. Have a discussion with the group about all the different things that people keep as mementos and possessions, such as prizes, gifts, certificates, books, records, ornaments, greetings cards, pictures, trophies, collectibles, musical instruments, holiday souvenirs, clothing and jewellery.

* NB: With this activity it is important that proper care is taken of peoples' objects. Not only does it show that you value them sharing that object and experience, but also that care is taken that it stays

with the owner. A nice way is to have some paper bags, and after the person has shared their memory, the co-worker writes the person's name on the bag, helps to place the object(s) in the bag, and returns it to the owner's safe-keeping.

Lucky dip

This is another variation on the idea of working with a broad range of objects. It is in the form of a guessing game, for those groups who enjoy a playful atmosphere. Find a cloth bag or suitably reminiscent bag in which to put a range of objects with a different texture and feel to them. Group members take a turn to reach inside the bag, have a good feel of all the objects, and then pick out something because it feels interesting, and they think they know what it is. They get the first chance to talk about the surprise object, and then everyone else in the group can contribute.

Making a collage of a few of our favourite things

This is a way for a group to make a visual record of some of the many things that they have been saying they liked in the sessions, such as special treats, food, film stars, singers, clothing, music, hobbies and interests. It can bring many different memories together in a composite collage, combining drawing, painting, photographs, pictures, text and all sorts of other materials such as fabrics and dried flowers to help represent the group members' favourite things. This activity takes a few sessions to work on, with group members all directly involved in choices about composition, form and content. There will be more ideas about specific themes for collages in Part 14.

The things my parents/grandparents used to say

A collection of favourite sayings

This involves making a written record of all the things that group members have recalled their parents and grandparents saying, such as advice, jokes, catchphrases, words of wisdom. Clearly, this is for groups whose members have shared such memories of their parents and grandparents in ways that have been enjoyable and entertaining for them. The written records need to be checked with the group members for their confirmation and agreement, and then typed up into an attractive and legible booklet for them. If there are not enough sayings related to parents and grandparents, this record could be extended to a general collection of favourite sayings and quotes – pearls of wisdom and humour to pass on to future generations.

Taking photographs

* This is a record of activity in the group, and also an activity in itself. You will need to consult your care home's policies and protocols on obtaining informed consent about taking and using photographs. Most importantly, the group members themselves must agree to it.

Group members can be photographed whilst engaging with the reminiscence objects, talking to others in the group, or taking part in any of the group activities. They can also take some photographs themselves of group activity. The resulting photographs can then be arranged on a canvas, framed and put on display in the home. This becomes another activity for the group. The photographs can also be scanned and made into a DVD slideshow for all the group members.

Getting ready for the special occasion

Throughout the year there is a series of holy days, festivals and events that group members may not only wish to celebrate, but also prepare for in the reminiscence group. The BBC Religion website has an interfaith calendar that is full of useful information about important days throughout the year for people of many different faiths. Depending on the time of the year, some of the group sessions may be held in good time to lead up to one of these events. These sessions could include activities related to cultural preparations for them, such as preparing food, making decorations, and learning about the history and true meaning and significance of these events in people's lives.

What makes a home a home?

✺ The idea of 'home' is central theme to mosts people's lives, although it may be a subject that some do not want to dwell on. If group members have been enjoying sharing memories about places in their lives that they considered home, then it is good to bring them together by listing with the group all of the things that a good home provides.

What you find is that eventually almost every other reminiscence theme emerges from the discussion, and it may lead to further work with the group on one of these consequent themes, such as Food, Work, Entertainment, Important People, Education, Health Care, Games, Hobbies and Special Occasions. You can ask the group to take you day by day through the weekly household routine, as a way of opening up the subject. This will not have been the same for every family. There will be interesting similarities and differences, as with all reminiscence.

Reminiscence crossword or word game

✺ This is for groups that like games and puzzles. The idea is not so much to get the answers right and win, although this may also be important for some, but to use the clues and answers as reminiscence prompts.

For example, questions could be related to any aspect of twentieth-century social history, such as cinema and popular entertainment. It is important not to get stuck on particular questions, but to use them to open up themes of interest. For example, the question 'Who starred in Singing in the Rain?' can then lead on to an invitation to start talking about films and cinema-going in general. The game is the prompt, not the be-all and end-all.

'The Reminiscence Puzzle Book 1930s to 1980s' by Robin Dynes contains many ideas for reminiscence puzzles. And, again, *The Daily Sparkle* and *The Weekly Sparkle* offers many games, puzzles and quizzes along these lines. You could also make up your own reminiscence quizzes specifically for the group, and play simple word-games such as Hangman, using reminiscence prompt words such as 'hopscotch', 'Eau de Cologne' or 'Frank Sinatra.'

Naming the group

In the development stage of the group, it is a good time to discuss with the group members what they would like the group to be called, other than just the 'Reminiscence Group.' This reinforces their ownership of the group, and helps to make the group feel unique. It also leads to an interesting discussion about the nature of the group from their point of view. Whatever they decide amongst themselves should be fully accepted, as long as all have been involved in the decision. We have had all manner of suggestions over the years – 'Memory Lane', 'Past Chronicles', 'Those Were The Days', 'I'd Forgotten I Could Remember That', and 'The Recycled Teenagers'. Age Exchange's two groups of senior actors called themselves 'The Good Companions' and 'The Memory Makers'. This idea may take a session or two to think about. After the decision has been made, the chosen name should be how the group is referred to.

Group anthems

This is connected with finding a name and an identity for the group. Some groups start and finish sessions by singing favourite songs. When the group members sing them together, they express their sense of belonging to the group. Sometimes they link arms and hold hands whilst singing them, so making the point even more clearly. This activity is a return to the idea of community singing, something that may have played a big part in people's social backgrounds, and helped to create a sense of community for them. There is no predicting what the songs will be.

* I can share some songs that became anthems for some of my groups, but this does not mean they will work for your group. You have to work through a good group process to get there. They were: 'Jerusalem', 'Come Round Any Old Time', 'Those Were The Days', 'I've Got Sixpence', 'Doing the Lambeth Walk', 'You'll Never Walk Alone', 'Que Sera Sera'.

Exercise — *Evaluating the development activity*

After running each of these activities, evaluate it and write a report according to the guidelines in Part 8. In addition to these general guidelines for evaluation, reply to the following specific questions.

- What evidence was there that this activity was appropriate for the group members?

- In what ways were the group members demonstrating greater confidence and trust in the group?
- Is this an activity that could be continued in future sessions? Are there more memories to share on that theme, or could the creative activity be repeated (e.g. more singing with different songs)?
- What other ideas for future activities emerged?

By the end of Part 10 trainees are expected to have:

- carried out and evaluated a selection of development activities that enable the group to focus on their identified themes and preferred activities.

In Part 11

In the concluding part of this section, we will look at the kinds of activities that can fit well with the final stage of a project.

PART 11 Activities During the Closing Stage

In Part 11 we will look at the kinds of activities that help to bring reminiscence projects to a positive and satisfying conclusion. They can also be interesting and enjoyable activities in their own right for groups in ongoing reminiscence sessions.

Completing work on group creative activity

If the group has taken on the task of producing something from their memories, then some of the final stage of the project can provide time for this work to be completed satisfactorily by the group so that it is ready for display and review. For example, we have already looked at creative ideas such as making a collage, making a collection of sayings, making a photo collage, writing about what 'home' is, and making a Memory Map. There will be many more ideas for reminiscence creative activities and products in Parts 12-17.

A book of memories

This is a written collection of some of the individual memories and stories that have come out of the group sessions. Collecting the material for it has to be done in close consultation with the group, requiring some work between sessions with individual group members to make sure that you have the correct details about the memories, and their permission to type them up. You can add some visual content to the booklet through the use of pictures or group members' own photographs, with their permission. Each group member can be given a copy of the booklet, and if you have everyone's permission it can also be put on display in the care home.

You can also make individual memory cards for each group member, containing some quotes from the sessions, with a photograph of them and with any images you have been able to find related to their shared memories.

Creating a reminiscence corner in the care home

This is a way of using the activities of the group to make an impact on the care environment. Objects and images that have arisen out of group activity and that you have obtained through research, donations or purchases, can be arranged to make an attractive and interesting display in the care home.

Compilation CD of favourite songs

If singing songs has been a regular group activity, then you may have accumulated enough material to make your own group album. You can make one of the sessions a recording session for the group, and then create your own CD. The case notes can include all the contributors, and the track listing can include captions related to why those songs were chosen and what memories were associated with them. A copy is given to each group member as a souvenir of the group.

End of project party

This can be a good way to celebrate the project, including ideas for party activities that have come out of the group sessions. It needs to be discussed and planned with the group members to ensure that it is what they want. Not everyone enjoys a party. If a party is what they would like, it can include group ideas for food and refreshment, background music, dancing, games and entertainment. Games we have played in final sessions have included a Lucky Dip of cheap and cheerful gifts, Pass the Parcel, dressing-up games, word games and quizzes, Consequences, and any other games that the group has enjoyed in the project. An old book or compendium of party games would be very useful for this.

Farewell songs

The party may be a good time to have a few songs with the group, even if singing has not played a big part in previous sessions. Ideas for suitable songs can be obtained from the group, and song sheets prepared for the final session. Songs can include those that represent the places group members come from, popular and well-known community songs, farewell songs and any songs that are particularly memorable for the group.

Presentations and thanks

The final session is the time to present to group members the records and products that have come out of the group activities. It can also be a time for more photographs of the presentations. Apart from being a record of the group and recognition of everyone's participation, it is also a great way for the reminiscence workers to show their thanks and appreciation for all the memories and contributions of the group members. We have looked at many ideas for presentation gifts, including individual memory cards, group memory booklets, DVD slideshows and compilation CDs of group singing.

Review

This is the time to reflect on the project as a whole, and have some discussion and feedback within the group on members' thoughts and feelings about the project. You can prepare a short review of the project, reminding the group and yourself of how the project started and developed, listing all the activities that the group took part in, and pointing out its achievements. Make sure that each individual is recognised as having played their part, by referring to some of their shared memories and other contributions.

Ideas for future activities

> "Every ending is a new beginning"
> Seneca

All through the project you have been looking forward with the group to future sessions, as you discover with them more about their interests and preferred activities. The end of the project should continue to have this positive forward-looking attitude. You will have a learned a great deal from your group about enjoyable activities for them in the future, outside of the reminiscence group. This can be checked with members at the final stage of the project, and ideas gathered for how they would like to spend their time in future. In this way the reminiscence project can enhance, enrich and have a positive influence on the rest of life in the care home, for example, mealtimes, special events, entertainment, parties, outings and other activity programmes. Your next project may be with another group of residents, but your group members from the last project can still be benefiting from the project outcomes.

Exercise *Evaluating the closing activity*

After you have run one of these activities, evaluate it and write a report according to the guidelines in Part 8. In addition to these general guidelines for evaluation, reply to the following specific questions.

- How did you ensure that the ending of the group was adequately prepared for, and that the work of the group was satisfactorily concluded?
- What positive outcomes for the group were reflected on and acknowledged?
- What ideas for future activities, events, outings and projects emerged from the ending of this group?

Exercise *Writing a final report*

- This is your task after the final session, working with your co-worker, and drawing from all your session plans and your notes from the post-session evaluation meetings. Your final report should be made available to the manager of your care home, and act as a record and assessment of what has been achieved in the project, including any difficulties or challenges that emerged and how you dealt with them.

The final report should include:

- A complete record of attendance
- Original aims and objectives for the group in general and for individual group members
- A list of all the sessions with a brief description of all the activities and themes used to open, develop and close each session
- A summary of the main discussion points in the evaluation meetings

- Any changes and adjustments made to aims and objectives as the project developed
- Evidence of social interaction in the group
- Quotes, memories and other contributions shared by individual group members
- Evidence of growth and development of the group as the project progressed
- Feedback on the individual sessions and overall project by the group members
- Your learning from this project, and what you might do differently next time
- Your project high points – the aspects of it that you regarded as particularly good pieces of work.

By the end of Part 11 trainees are expected to have:

- acquired an understanding of how to carry out and evaluate a selection of activities that help to bring reminiscence projects to a satisfactory conclusion. N.B. These activities may as yet not be appropriate for the groups that you are running.
- acquired an understanding of how to write a final reminiscence project report.

The next section, Parts 12-17

- Parts 12 to 17 will look at reminiscence and creative activities. In Part 12 we will explore the relationship between reminiscence and creativity, the issues involved in creating reminiscence-based arts products, and how to nurture the creativity of your residents.

SECTION 3 • REMINISCENCE AND CREATIVE ACTIVITIES • PARTS 12 – 17

PART 12 — *Reminiscence and Creativity*

Introduction

* Parts 12–17 will provide many ideas for using a variety of creative activities to help people express their reminiscences.

* What is creativity? It is quite a tricky thing to define, beyond the meaning of making or producing something, or bringing something into being. It's a matter of how you do it, what you produce, and the effects it has on people.

Exercise — *What is creativity?*

> List some activities that and your friends and colleagues consider to be 'creative'. What are the characteristic qualities and features of these 'creative' activities? Do not restrict your list to the creative arts: broaden it out to include more everyday types of creative activity at home or work, and also appreciation of creativity in others, e.g. gardening, and listening to music

Creativity and positive outcomes from reminiscence

How can creativity help us to achieve the benefits that we are aiming for in our work? Reminiscence in itself can be viewed as a creative activity. It is to some extent a re-creation of one's past experiences. If it is shared with others, it has to take some form or other, and there are many different forms that it might take.

Our role is to help people find the best way of expressing their memories, taking into account their abilities, talents and preferred ideas for activities. Once group members have found stories about their lives that have been received well in the group, they may then want to share them with a wider audience, using another form of creative process to produce something that can be shown to others. The shared memories can have an inspirational effect on them and on those around them. These creative ideas cannot be imposed on group members, but come from the heart of themselves.

✸ The ideas for creative activities in Parts 12–17 have been successful because group members have seen them as a way of further exploring, expressing and enjoying their memories.

A lack of confidence and the use of intimidating language (such as 'creative art forms') may hinder creativity. The emphasis must be on the value of people and their stories, and on a beneficial process. At its simplest, creativity can be defined as making something, and then presenting it to others. This can be done using music, literature, drama, painting or craftwork, or it can be done with more everyday activities, for example, listening to music, looking at pictures, chatting over tea, reading a newspaper. All of these foster creativity. The important factor is to match the right activity to the right person and their memories.

Individual or group activity

Any of the activities in this guide can be used with individuals or with groups. In earlier parts we have looked at reasons why people may prefer either group or one-to-one reminiscing, and it is important to be aware of this, and to offer people both when you can. Some people may need one-to-one work before they feel confident enough to join group activities. Some people may need one-to-one work when they have developed an individual interest beyond the group activities, for example, to produce a Life Story Book. As always, it is a question of respecting individual choice and meeting individual needs.

Activity   *Reminiscence portraits*

✸ This activity blends writing and visual arts ideas in order to enhance and add value to the person and their memories. This can be done in small groups or one-to-one.

The method is to collect a variety of reminiscence quotes or sound bites from participants, and then to work towards placing these around a central image on a framed canvas.

The resulting portrait can then be displayed somewhere in the care home (with the person's consent). It is best done with group members who have already begun sharing memories and who are relaxed about the process, rather than as an opening activity.

Explain the aims and methods of the activity. Then explore four different broad reminiscence topics with the participants: Special Places, Special People, Special Times of Life, and Life Values.

Open up these topics and invite people to make comments about them, and to start thinking about memories they would like to choose, and how they would like to express them. When they have made their choices, you can start writing these down word for word in the way the person wants it to be expressed.

The visual aspects of the portrait are the choice of the central image (not an easy choice), the style of lettering, decisions about the colour and shape of the canvas, and the choice of frame. There are also important considerations about how the different memories can be positioned and related to each other on the canvas.

It seems like quite a simple creative idea, but in fact is complex, and can be problematic. It may require some time and thought before people are sure about what they want to contribute, let alone how they want it to be presented.

Exercise — *Evaluating the activity*

Obtain feedback from each participant on the process involved in this activity.

- What did they enjoy? What did they find difficult or challenging? To what extent did they achieve their objectives for taking part?
- How involved did they feel in the creative process and the product? What support and assistance did you offer them that proved helpful to the task at hand?
- What were their views on the final product? Was the activity adequately resourced in terms of time, personnel and materials? What may have helped to achieve better outcomes?

What were your key learning points?

Creativity in later life

There are unfortunately many negative stereotypical views about what older people are capable of and even about what is appropriate for them. Such views limit the possibilities that should be open to them. The evidence shows that not only is continuing creativity possible in old age, but that it may also be the time for development of new creative styles, or it may be the time for new creative interests. A number of factors may contribute to this: the insights provided over the course of a long life, more time being available for imaginative activities, increased independence of mind, relative freedom from daily work demands, and the perspective of someone approaching the end of the long journey of life. There may also be creative responses to the challenges of ageing, such as age-related illnesses or the crises of life-threatening illnesses. As with all of us at any age, we need helpful and supportive social and health care systems around us in order to assist our drive towards development and self-expression.

Nurturing creativity in the care home

Person-centred care emphasises what people can do, not what they cannot do. It is important to have a positive and open attitude to what your residents are capable of. Never underestimate older people's potential creativity. They may have been creative throughout their lives, and now only lack the motivation or means of expression in order to be creative again. The care home can be a place where that creativity is reawoken and developed.

Your residents will need different kinds and levels of support and assistance to help them achieve what they want. Some may need you simply to obtain their materials for them; some may need you to work with them to create the finished products; some may need you to do most of the work under their direction. Our role is to assist their creativity as far as possible, and to help them get the most from their reminiscences.

Arts-based reminiscence products and a beneficial process

> "Look after the process, and the product will look after itself"

The process is key to the success of any creative activity leading to an arts-based product. If the process is not beneficial and effective in helping participants achieve their aims, then the product will not be satisfactory. One of our mottos at Age Exchange is 'Look after the process, and the product will look after itself.' Even if it is not a finished product – that is, more creative work could have been done with more time and resources – then it is more important to respect the pace of work and people's ownership of it, and appreciate it as work in progress, rather than impose an unnatural finish to it with the activities organisers taking it over.

★ The principles of good practice in reminiscence work, as covered in Parts 3–5, must be adhered to throughout every creative reminiscence activity. If not, you may end up with a beautiful arts product that means little to the participants.

Interpersonal skills more important than arts and craft skills

Your most important skills in doing this work are the interpersonal skills and qualities that enable you to provide good person-centred care to people. Arts and craft skills may be useful, especially if participants want to attempt a challenging product, but these are supplementary rather than essential. It is more important when planning and providing activities that people's individual needs, skills and interests are taken into account throughout the process, and that they are valued and supported in whatever creative activity they should choose to express themselves. I recommend Tessa Perrin's chapter on 'Towards a New Culture' in *The New Culture of Therapeutic Activity with Older People* (Speechmark) for a more in-depth presentation of new positive approaches to care and activity provision for older people.

By the end of Part 12 trainees are expected to have:

★ made a list of various activities that are considered to be creative, and identified their characteristic qualities

★ acquired an understanding of how creativity can be linked to reminiscence in order to achieve positive outcomes

★ carried out and evaluated the 'Reminiscence Portraits' activity

★ acquired an understanding of the potential for creativity in later life, and the role of the care home, activities organiser and care staff in nurturing creativity.

In Part 13

Next time we will focus on ideas for linking reminiscence with various forms of writing activities.

PART 13 Writing Activities

Introduction

✹ In this part we will explore a variety of ways in which reminiscences can be written down in order to develop them, record them, and make a creative product inspired by them. Some of these activities combine writing with other forms of creativity, such as photography, drama, storytelling and music.

Making lists

This is a simple way of starting to write down memories as remembered examples of a particular topic (as already described in Part 10 with regard to games and play). As group members share memories on a theme you write these up on a flip chart, and the growing list acts as a visual and verbal trigger for you and the group. More examples of such lists could include perfumes, fabrics, food, famous people, singers, actors, household chores, recipes, home remedies. Much of what is shared in a group can be easily forgotten if you rely upon your memory after the group session to recall it. Making lists is a productive way of prompting memories, recording them and having them as a resource for future work.

✹ As the project progresses, you may find more information on some of the listed items, and begin to create thematic booklets on some of the above topics, along the lines of the 'Collection of favourite sayings' in Part 10.

Using objects to write a short story

Unpacking a handling collection – choosing objects and creating a group story from them – is a combination of a game, imaginative storytelling and creative writing, all to some extent or other influenced by reminiscence. For example, someone picks a skipping rope and says, "One day as I was skipping in the backyard, my friend came round to see me." The next person picks a camera, and says, "My friend was a keen photographer, and asked me to go into town for the day with her to take some photographs," and so on. Someone in the group writes down the story as it develops from object to object. The story ends when the group agrees that it has come to an end.

Anthology of reminiscences

As described in Part 11 you can put together a written collection of memories coming from the group, and once you have worked with a number of different groups, you will have collected a large amount of material that could be put together in the form of an anthology of reminiscences. The challenge is how to arrange and present all these different stories so that they come across well. You could arrange them chronologically, as an unfolding story of life in the twentieth century, or you could edit them thematically, so that you have chapters on different themes such as Home Life, Work, Play, Entertainment, Health and Education. It is also a good idea to illustrate the memories where you can with contributors' own photographs (with their permission) or relevant images that you have collected yourself.

An anthology of favourite poems

There are many classic collections of verse, such as *Palgrave's Golden Treasury* and the *Oxford Book of English Verse*. This is a chance for your group to choose their own selection of best poems and edit their own classic anthology of verse. You may find Pam Ayres alongside Shakespeare, and Stanley Holloway next to Wordsworth. That's as it should be. A short introduction to each poem by the contributors would make this collection distinctive.

Individual themed written reminiscences

> "Writing comes more easily if you have something to say"
> Sholem Asch

For the group members who like to go away after the group and write down some memories, there will be many possible subjects for them to consider from the activity within the group. You could highlight these for them in the closure of the session. A few examples are: my special day, a typical day at work, my first job, the holiday of a lifetime, a magic moment, a letter of advice to those about to get married from one who knows, the secret of a long and happy life. This is a kind of autobiographical writing, done with a reader in mind. Some residents may need help with this, so that you act as a scribe for them.

Journeys of a lifetime

A group travelogue

This is not just a theme for group members who have travelled to distant countries, but takes into account all the different types of journeys we make in life in order to lead our lives. Holidays are just one reason for travelling – there are all the other reasons as well, such as work, play, education, family, friends, entertainment, food and drink, health care and shopping. Our role is to explore themes in depth and breadth, thus helping group members to realise that they are included in this subject: the tram journey into town, the bicycle ride to the picnic, the bus to the cinema, the walk to school, and the flight to New York are all part of this subject, and make for interesting links and contrasts between group members. Why do we travel, and why are these journeys important to us?

Ask group members to describe the different types of transport involved, and recall the sensory experiences of the journeys – the sights, sounds, textures, tastes and smells of travelling. This subject can lead on to all sorts of other themes of interest as group members recall both the unusual and the everyday journeys that they have made in their lives. As with all reminiscence themes, there will be a mixture of good and bad memories of journeys for group members to choose from. Sometimes, the nightmare stories can bring the greatest mirth now that it's all done with, but clearly that is a choice only the person whose memory it is can make. There will also be some fascinating comparisons and contrasts between the way people travelled in the past and travel nowadays.

Life story books

This is a collection of the different stories and reminiscences that an individual person has shared about their lives, put into a form that can be shared with others of that person's choosing. It is something that they give you authority to do with them, and the final product belongs to them. The process must adhere to principles of good practice in reminiscence work, especially regarding confidentiality and permission to use material.

There are many issues about how to organise and present the material, whether thematically or chronologically. The most important consideration is that the final product is meaningful for the person and works well as a memory trigger for them in the future. The use of suitable illustrations, textures and scents will enhance the value of the life-story book as a continuing source of reminiscence prompts for the person. You may need to do some research on behalf of the person, searching for images of places that they have remembered. The book can also include up-to-date information about enjoyable interests and activities in the present. It helps to use a format that enables you to add to the material as and when you obtain it.

Captions for museum exhibitions

People's shared reminiscences are a vital part of our heritage, and the museum services need such material to breathe life into their permanent and occasional exhibitions on various aspects of living history. Museum objects, documents and images have a deeper significance when placed beside a quote from someone who lived and felt that experience. Age Exchange has produced exhibitions on many reminiscence themes such as Local History, the Second World War, Going to the Cinema, Christmas, the Merchant Navy, The London Docklands, the Windrush, Children at Play, Summer Holidays. Such reminiscences are often in the form of short captions and sound-bites, but also available in extended versions for students who want to go into more depth.

Transcribed and edited interviews

If someone has a large amount to say on a given subject, or if they want a life-history interview, then this needs to be done outside the group, and adequate time provided for it. The person might want this to be off the record, or might be pleased for it to be recorded, in which case you may have an hour's worth of material to be transcribed and edited. You will find out more on conducting individual interviews, transcribing and editing in Part 22 on Reminiscence and Oral History.

Writing a group poem

It often produces a mixture of disbelief and consternation when I suggest to a group that we could write a poem together on a subject. For many people it is something that either they have never tried or when they did try, they felt it was a total failure. This is a very different way of writing a poem, based on reminiscences that people have been sharing in the group, and being a team effort. I describe poetry to the group as 'memorable words – words that make an impact on us through their sound, rhythm and meaning.' Their memories have already had an impact in the group. This is the process for writing the poem.

- Agree on a reminiscence theme.
- Each person writes or dictates two lines of poetry on that theme.
- The group comes together to listen to each other's lines.
- The group decides in what order the lines should go.
- The group discusses any changes that might improve the poem.
- The group agrees on the final form of the poem, and a title for it.
- One of the group reads the poem aloud.

Random sensory poem

A day at the seaside

Go through each of the senses. Ask group members what they can see, hear, touch, taste and smell at the seaside. And what do they do at the seaside? For example, you can see 'the big blue sea', 'the Punch and Judy Show', and the 'white horse waves'. Make a list of all the answers to these questions. Cut up and fold up each answer, and put them in a box like raffle tickets. Go round the group and each person picks a piece of paper with a word or phrase. The poem is composed in the order in which the pieces of paper and phrases are picked.

Writing song lyrics

You can think with the group about setting their memories as lyrics to well-known melodies. This is for groups that already have done work on poems and songs, and have shown a playful interest in being creative with them. For example, 'Show me the way to Southend. I'm cycling all the way from West Ham' (to the tune of 'Show Me The Way to Go Home'). This could be a lot of fun for the group, or it might be an inspirational choice of new words for a melody. Another idea is to compile lyrics as lists of things remembered, as in Ian Dury's song 'Reasons To Be Cheerful'.

Scripts for theatre productions

This has been a special area of interest for Age Exchange. Reminiscences can provide excellent source material for dramatisation. It is for those group members who want to work towards a theatre production or short piece of drama based on the memories that have been shared in a reminiscence project. There are lots of choices to be made about which stories to dramatise, which material to use, and casting.

Is this something that you will re-enact for the group, or will they participate in the acting as well? It requires much thought and work for participants and workers to be faithful to the reminiscence and to make it dramatic. Part 16 looks at ideas for linking reminiscence with drama activities.

Exercise

Evaluating the writing activity

Obtain feedback from each participant on the process involved in this writing activity.

- What did they enjoy? What did they find difficult or challenging?
- To what extent did they achieve their objectives for taking part?
- What evidence was there that the writing activity assisted their reminiscence process?
- How involved did they feel in the writing process and the product? What support and assistance did you offer them that proved helpful to the task at hand?
- What were their views on the final product?
- Was the activity adequately resourced in terms of time, personnel and materials? What may have helped to achieve better outcomes?
- What were your key learning points?

By the end of Part 13 trainees are expected to have:

- acquired an understanding of how writing activities can be used to help people achieve positive outcomes from their reminiscences
- carried out and evaluated a selection of reminiscence activities using writing.

In Part 14

We will look at how to link reminiscence with visual arts activities.

PART 14 Visual Arts Activities

✻ In this part, we will explore a variety of ways in which reminiscences can be presented visually in order to develop them, record them and make a creative product inspired by them. Some of these activities combine visual arts activities with other forms of creativity, such as writing, drama, storytelling and music.

Drawing from memory

"A picture paints a thousand words"

Someone does a sketch diagram of something that the person is describing visually from their memory. In Part 5 we looked at Special Places for this activity, but it could be something more specific such as the living room, the view from a window, types of clothing, an important person, the local theatre, a favourite meal, or anything that someone is giving you a mental picture of.

If you need to do the drawing for them, do not attempt a realistic portrayal of the thing or person being described; it would be impossible anyway. Focus on the main remembered details that the person is telling you – the colour, size, shape, position and main characteristics of things. The person can then think of a title for it, and use it to tell the group the story behind it.

Wonderful moments

There are lots of ideas for what you might draw with, or for, someone that are based on a memory of the good things and moments in life. They may have been recalling moments when everything went well, when they felt a great sense of peace and security, when they appreciated something very beautiful, or when they felt very close and intimate with someone they loved. There may be a picture or image of something that represents this joyful moment. If they would like you to draw it for them, do so carefully and lovingly with them, paying close attention to their details, and accepting totally non-critically what it was about this moment that was so special for them. There may be some background music they can remember that would perfectly accompany this moment, acting as the soundtrack for the picture. The last part of the activity is for them to entitle it, and then use it as an aid to their description of their wonderful moment.

Memory map

This builds on the 'Mapping special places' activity as described in Part 3. That was more of an opening activity, whereas this takes the process a stage further to the creation of a map with pictures of special places and captions of related memories that can be framed and displayed in the care home.

This may require time and effort, and a little expense searching for non-copyrighted images on the internet of the places that the group members have recalled. Obtain a few different pictures so that they can make a choice, and then find out from them their related memory of the place, adding this as the caption to the image on the map, and attributing it to the person whose memory it is.

Connect up all the images and captions to the places on the map that they refer to, using coloured ribbon or tape.

Group drawing or painting

If there is an overarching theme that connects all the drawings or paintings being produced by group members, then they could all be collected, cut to size and arranged together in a composite group picture, that is then framed and displayed in the care home. Subjects that have led to such group compositions have included changing fashions, street scenes, the home, festivals, the neighbourhood, the kitchen and the great outdoors.

Reconstruction of the old High Street

This is for a local group that has been sharing recollections of the way the local high street has changed over the years. As the group members recall more of the shops, buildings, landmarks and other amenities that are no longer there, you can draw with them a map of the High Street as it used to be, highlighting the special places that only exist now in their memories.

With these hands

This is for a group that has been recalling all the various types of work and giving that they have done throughout their lives. You draw around their hands to get an outline of them, and write inside the hands, fingers and thumbs the different memories that they have shared in relation to the topic. This is quite an intimate activity, and the group members would have to feel comfortable about allowing you to carry it out with them.

Where have your feet been?

This may feel more comfortable for some than the previous activity, and is the same idea, except that the focus is on the topic of travel and mobility. You draw around people's feet to get an outline of them, and write the journeys they made in their lives. As with 'The journeys of a lifetime' activity in Part 13, open up the topic so that it is about more than long journeys to faraway places, but includes all the journeys we have made in order to live our lives, for example, the walk to school, the journey to work, the day-trip to Brighton, the tram to town, the visit to relations and the bus to the swimming pool.

Making a collage

A day at the seaside

This activity might suit a group that has come together on the theme of spending a day at the seaside. It lends itself to making a collage, because of the sensory nature of the subject, and the likelihood that a large amount of visual information will present itself from people's memories of the experience. The collage may make use of a background of sand, sea and sky, and place details on top of this such as lobster pots, sandcastles, buckets and spades, seaweed, sailing boats, clouds, seagulls, etc. Group members may also want to add to the collage any written memories, poems or songs that remind them of the seaside.

Gallery of assets

Certificates of achievements

This is an idea for paying tribute to the too-often neglected achievements of people throughout the courses of their lives. Draw some attractive frames around the page – the types used for presenting prizes and awards. Ask the person what lifetime achievements, abilities, assets and strengths of character they would like to represent in the frames. Can they think of an object to draw inside the frame to represent the achievement or asset? For example, a tool might represent work and endeavour, or a clock could represent patience. If it is an abstract quality for which they cannot think of any image, then simply write the name of the positive quality inside the frame.

❈ This is a further activity for those who have been freely recalling and sharing positive aspects of their character in previous activities. It is not something to try with someone who may have difficulty in so doing.

Important people in my life

Photo album

This is a development of the Reminiscence Portraits activity described in Part 12. This focuses on the important people in a person's life – the people who helped, supported, guided and inspired them at different times in their lives. Apart from family members, they could include work colleagues, school or college friends, teachers, mentors, role models, icons, heroes and heroines, or even a stranger who once showed kindness. They could include people in the present as well as the past. Represent the person with a photograph, drawing or suitable image inside a picture frame, and write down the way in which that person was helpful and supportive. What might be a typical quote from that person to you? Throughout the reminiscence sessions group members are often reminded of important people in their lives by the objects on display, and these might be suitable images to represent them.

Making a photo collage

This is an activity mentioned at the end of the 'Taking photographs' activity in Part 10. As well as using photographs of group members involved in group activities, you may have obtained permission to make copies of some of the group members' own personal photographs. You may also have collected some non-copyrighted photographic images from the internet, related to the memories that have been shared within the group. This provides you with a wealth of photographic material with which to consider making a photo collage with the group. There is quite an art to this process, deciding which images to use, how to edit them, how to compose the collage, and how to arrange and position the different photographs. The key factor is the involvement of the group members in the choices made, if not in the actual execution of it.

Life story photo or picture album

In Part 13 we looked at the issues concerning the making of 'Life story books' as principally a writing activity. For some people, the emphasis on text would be an inappropriate way of presenting their memories, as written language is not so meaningful for them now. There may also be questions of taste and preference for visual imagery over language that would make a photo or picture album a more effective end product for the person.

Painting a backdrop

This is a visual arts activity to support a reminiscence show by creating a painting of memories from the show to be used as a backdrop for the performance. This activity could involve residents who are acting in the show, or it could include those who contributed some stories or were inspired by stories from the show, but who do not want to act in it. This would involve painting on large panels clearly visible to the audience, and creating large images that act as memory triggers and prompts for the performers. As with all group creations, there are interesting and challenging creative decisions to be made about how best to present and arrange the material from the show.

Exercise — *Evaluating the visual arts activity*

Obtain feedback from each participant on the process involved in this visual arts activity.

- What did they enjoy? What did they find difficult or challenging?
- To what extent did they achieve their objectives for taking part?
- What evidence was there that the visual arts activity assisted their reminiscence process?
- How involved did they feel in the visual arts process and the product? What support and assistance did you offer them that proved helpful to the task at hand?

- What were their views on the final product?
- Was the activity adequately resourced in terms of time, personnel and materials? What may have helped to achieve better outcomes?
- What were your key learning points?

By the end of Part 14 trainees are expected to have:

* acquired an understanding of how to use visual arts activities to help people achieve positive outcomes from their reminiscences

* carried out and evaluated a selection of reminiscence activities using the visual arts.

In Part 15

We will look at how to link reminiscence with music activities.

PART 15   Music Activities

Introduction

Music is a powerful memory trigger, and a very effective way of creating a mood and an ambience in reminiscence groups. The challenges are how to find the right music, and how to use it to best effect.

> "Without music, life would be a mistake"
> Nietzsche

There may be an issue regarding the legality of playing copyrighted CDs and other recordings in care settings other than residential or nursing care homes. If you are uncertain, check this with your manager.

Overtures

- As group members are entering the room and finding their seats, playing some background music can help to create a relaxed and pleasant ambience.

Setting this up may require some trial and error at the start of projects, until you find out from the group what kind of music works best as a way of creating a welcoming and settling atmosphere for them. Whilst the music is playing, you can say your hellos to the group members as they come in, talk a little about today's session, and also discuss what kind of music it would be nice to play at the start of sessions.

Shall we dance?

If someone seems to be enjoying a piece of music and is swinging their arms or moving their feet in time to it, then you can ask the person if they would like to have a dance with you. Of course, while some people never dance, others love to dance, so it is a case of getting to know the group members. If you don't ask, you won't know. People who are unable to walk can be invited to dance with their arms.

Healthy moves

This follows on from games like 'Charades' and 'What's my line'? There may have been a number of remembered movements and actions that have emerged from group activities, and these can be put together as a series of gentle exercises. For example, mimes of ironing, hanging up the washing, using the mangle, throwing jacks up in the air and catching them, swinging a skipping rope and playing conkers. It is a question of picking up on movements that group members have shown that they can remember and do. Discuss with the group what music to use to accompany the sequence of movements.

Listening to music

Just listening – no need to do any other type of activity. Let the words and music have their effect – some people may want to get up and dance, some may want to move their hands and feet. (I'm reminded of a man who started waving his arms as if he had a football scarf on the terraces to 'You'll Never Walk Alone'.)

Singing

We have already discussed this in Part 10, when we looked at the importance of group anthems and community singing. Some groups may very much appreciate the opportunity to come together as a chorus from time to time, and sing together songs that they grew up with and used to sing with family, friends and neighbours. Part of the work of the group can be to find what these songs could be for the group members. This will depend on their age and cultural background. Once you have your list, then make song sheets for the group, so that they have the words in front of them should they need them. This can happen as a way of starting or finishing the session, or if very popular with the group, it could be the main activity.

Around the gramophone

This requires a record player in good working condition, and some records of music that the group have said that they would like to hear. Fortunately, most vinyl and 78rpm records are very low-cost. It would be nice to have an original old gramophone that group members recognise, but there are also some very good relatively inexpensive modern retro record players available. The good thing about this activity is that it helps to recreate the feeling of being with your friends, and listening to your favourite music together.

However, I do recall one lady who said to me, "What a shame that you haven't got a CD player!"

Desert Island Discs

This has proved a popular activity with groups, probably because it is such a familiar format for so many people, as it is based on the long-running BBC radio programme. It's a way of giving people time to think about their favourite music and also reflecting on the times of life that the music recalls. If they were on a desert island, which pieces of music or songs would they like to be able to listen to in their solitude? What would remind them of important people, places and times in their lives? What would give them joy and pleasure to hear? It may take some time to make this selection, and it would be assisted by using various memory triggers that give them choices – records, photographs of singers, music programmes and a selection of different types of music to listen to. After you have found the group members' Desert Island Discs, you can search for them at your nearest best CD shop and return with them for your own group version of the famous radio programme.

Music venues

This is an activity that might help people to locate their musical memories. It can be difficult to answer the question, "What is your favourite music?" Sometimes we have to use a more indirect approach. This is another listing activity, using a flip chart to write up all the musical venues that people can remember from their lives – the places in their lives where they have heard music. You may need to start the ball rolling by suggesting some possible types of places, such as school, concert halls, special occasions, scouts and guides, at home or going out for the evening.

Local songs

* This activity may be associated with work you have done on the places where the residents come from – where they were born and bred, where they consider home.

Are there any songs that are about or associated with those places? For example, 'Maybe It's Because I'm A Londoner,' 'The Town I Loved So Well' (Derry), 'The Lambeth Walk', 'New York, New York', 'Santa Lucia' (Naples), 'Liverpool Lou' and 'Island in the Sun' (the Caribbean). The songs need not mention the place by name, but by its style, mood and character may remind people of these places. Of course, just because a song is about a place where somebody comes from, this does not mean they are going to want to listen to it or sing it. As always, no assumptions can be made... and we need to find out from people themselves.

Television and radio theme tunes

There are various CD compilations of classic television and radio theme tunes going back to the 1930s. They can contribute to a session working on the theme of entertainment, or they can help to set the scene for memories related to a particular time, as the music and the programmes are so evocative of their time. Once again such an activity is not a test, but rather a memory trigger that may have all kinds of different associations for people.

Songs my parents and grandparents used to sing

This is a development from the idea of collecting sayings and catchphrases that we remember our parents and grandparents using. What were the songs that they loved to sing? It cannot be taken for granted that people themselves will like the songs of their parents, but it may be a source of pleasure for them and another way of honouring their forebears. You may need to obtain the lyrics for the group, and hand out song sheets for them to sing the songs as a chorus. As suggested earlier, you could then make a CD recording of the group singing these songs, and give everyone a copy.

Reminiscence skiffle band

This harks back to the days of skiffle when people used homemade musical instruments to make their own music. Just about any household object could be used to make a percussive instrument, such as a washboard, jug, bucket or jelly mould. These are the kinds of objects that you will have been gathering together for your reminiscence handling collection. You could use other instruments as well, such as castanets, rattles, bells, whistles and coconut halves.

This could be a fun activity for a group that had already indicated they liked music and physical activity. The group members choose the music that they want to play along to, and then pick their homemade instruments from your collection. It probably best suits a lively up-tempo piece of music with a strong rhythm, and something very familiar to the group. We had great fun recently with one group playing along to the William Tell Overture and the theme tune to 'Steptoe and Son'.

Music composition

Some group members may be able to play musical instruments, and have some experience of composing their own music. With support, they may be able to write new pieces of music inspired by their memories coming from the group sessions, or the memories of other group members. This idea is included because it makes the point that there should be no limits to the creative potential of our group members. There have been some interesting music composition projects with people living with dementia. Some specialised knowledge of this field would help to nurture your residents' latent musical creativity.

Closing songs

Certain kinds of songs are about saying 'farewell' or 'au revoir', and so are good ways of bringing a session to a close, or indeed bringing a project to a close. There is a danger of overdoing this by singing a long list of goodbye songs that can have a rather maudlin effect on the group. So include other songs that the group knows and loves as well.

Exercise — *Evaluating the music activity*

Obtain feedback from each participant on the process involved in this music activity.

- What did they enjoy? What did they find difficult or challenging?
- To what extent did they achieve their objectives for taking part?
- What evidence was there that the music activity assisted their reminiscence process?
- How involved did they feel in the musical process and the product? What support and assistance did you offer them that proved helpful to the task at hand?
- What were their views on the final product?

- Was the activity adequately resourced in terms of time, personnel and materials? What may have helped to achieve better outcomes?
- What were your key learning points?

By the end of Part 15 trainees are expected to have:

✳ acquired an understanding of how to use music to help people achieve positive outcomes from their reminiscences

✳ carried out and evaluated a selection of reminiscence activities using music

In Part 16

We will look at how to link reminiscence with drama activities.

PART 16 Drama Activities

Introduction

Producing drama from memories is an exciting and empowering option for participants in reminiscence projects. It is vital that the basic principles of good practice in reminiscence work are adhered to throughout the process, and that the drive to undertake drama does not induce the practitioners to take any short cuts. We emphasise 'respect for choice' at every stage, and speak not so much of theatre and dramatisation, but more of 'showing' and 'sharing' memories with others. Movement and performance are actually very natural developments in reminiscence that may require little or no stimulation or prompting by the facilitators.

Sculpt a treasured object

- This has worked well with groups that have used mime and movement in other sessions to express themselves, such as in the 'What's my line?' game or playing 'Charades'.

It is also related to 'Bring a thing', being a way to help people think about important objects in their lives. Group members may recall some objects they have kept that are important to them; they may also think of possessions they once had that have become lost, and which they miss.

They are invited to show the group what the object looked like by using their hands to shape it and indicate its size, weight and texture. They can also describe it with words to give it more detail, and tell the group where it came from, how they got it and why it is important to them.

What if we were there now?

- This is a simple yet powerful suggestion that lends itself to memories that take us back to places in the past that have a distinct atmosphere of their own.

When we reminisce, we sometimes produce vivid descriptions of these places for ourselves and others, and this can be picked up on and developed by asking further detailed questions about the place - the sights, sounds, smells, tastes, textures and activities of the place. Certain things will stand out more than others. The key point here is to be sure that these are places that people have freely chosen to go back to in their memories, and that they are getting something positive out of it. This activity helps to set the scene for any kind of play-acting or drama that might develop from the memories. Remembered places might include the park, the beach, a train compartment, a children's playground, a dance hall, the cinema, a family mealtime, the classroom, the office, the tram, the street, the textile mill: the list is endless.

Show me round your home

✳ When a participant is trying to remember more detail about a place where they once lived, this activity has proved helpful in prompting more memories.

Invite them to imagine that they are standing somewhere in their old home, and that you are there with them. Find out exactly where you are, and then ask them to show you round the rest of their home. Ask them to walk around the imagined home with you, and to tell you what it looks like, and any other memories that they want to share about it. As with all these activities, any sign that the person is uncertain or uncomfortable about doing it is a clear indication that it is not right for them, either as an activity or possibly as a topic. We have observed some remarkable feats of memory by some people doing this activity, helping them to reconstruct their old family abode for an audience, but, more importantly, also obtaining much personal satisfaction and happiness from recalling a place so dear to their hearts.

Take me with you

This is simply asking someone who is remembering a journey to take you with them on that journey – that is, describe it in detail and everything that it involved. This could be something challenging such as climbing a mountain, or something less demanding such as going to the cinema. Rather than simply talking about the journey, this activity involves movement around the room as if the journey were actually being undertaken. The addition of movement and imagination to the activity aids the memory and instantly gives it dramatic potential.

Going shopping

Many people (though by no means all) would agree that the days when the customer was king are over. What was it about going to the shops that made it so much better an experience for the shopper? Find out some of the ways in which shop assistants looked after and treated their customers well (or not!), and re-enact these scenes with someone playing the part of the customer, and someone the shop assistant. Being true to the memories will produce authentic little scenes.

May I have this dance?

We are at the dance hall in our imaginations, and you need to be instructed by the experts in the group as to the correct way to ask somebody for a dance. You can role-play this yourself, trying several approaches to the group members until they agree that you have got it just right.

The household weekly routine

This is a performance piece based on all the different types of housework that the group has remembered (only if they want to!). It can make an interesting central scene for a reminiscence show, taking us through all the days of the week, and dramatically representing time passing in the characters' lives.

Through the day and night

This is like the above performance piece, but instead of taking us through the typical week it takes us through the typical day and night at a certain time in people's lives. This can make an engaging and visually stimulating introduction to a reminiscence show, introducing us to all the characters before we get to know them better in the play.

Short scenes from life

> "There never was yet an uninteresting life. Such a thing is an impossibility"
> Mark Twain

Drama is conflict and tension followed by resolution. So you can listen to memories to see if they have this quality about them. Here are some examples of short dramatic scenes that we have worked on with people in groups. The emphasis is on having fun in these short snappy scenes, rather than exploring intense and powerful emotions in great depth.

Late home

This plays out the perennial debate about what time young people should be back home after a night out.

The strict teacher

Discipline in the classroom is another subject that never leaves us, and this explores the lines that schoolchildren and teachers had to walk.

The job interview

Will the interviewee get the job or not?

Teach me your job

This is a good way of putting the older people in the position of experts and teachers, and we, the activities organisers, are the pupils and students. It's your first day on the job, and the group members have to show you the ropes.

Playing games

When we start to play remembered games that we have not played for some time, then we go back into the roles, times and places of the past, and naturally begin to recreate memories. Playground, street and party games evoke the past and create a lot of fun.

* This is an example of when reminiscence can become play and acting without anyone needing to introduce the idea of drama. Games are to be played, not talked about.

Bringing the photograph to life

This drama idea follows on from 'Looking at photographs' and 'Bring a thing'. If someone has recalled a photograph that they had of an enjoyable group experience with family or friends, or if they have brought it to show the group, then you and group members can recreate this moment by playing the parts of people in the photograph. The person whose photograph it is must understand what is being suggested, and want to do it wholeheartedly. They have the final decision on all aspects of this activity: casting, content, style and form. The aim is to recreate some of the enjoyment and pleasure gained from what was a good social experience for them, and to learn more about the kinds of social occasions that they enjoy.

Dressing up

Bring in a selection of hats, gloves, scarves and bags for the group members to look at and try on. Once they have made their selection, they can remain dressed up for a while. This works well if it is linked with a theme that the group has been working on, such as going out to the cinema or dancing. You can ask them where they would be, or where they would be going, dressed up like that. They may become their younger selves or they may take on the role of some other character.

Posing for the camera

This could follow on from dressing up and imagining that we are in other times and places. With permission, take photographs of the group members, and ask them to pose for the camera. Do not ask them to pose in any particular way. Let them choose for themselves whether they pose dramatically or in an understated way. Some people take this opportunity to start acting in character and playing to the camera.

If you'd only had a camera

* This is an imaginative activity that has helped to create some powerful scenes for reminiscence shows. We have all had times in our lives when we wish we'd had a camera in order to capture the moment.

Such times may be when you met up with old friends, family reunions, visiting beautiful places, special occasions, comical moments, unusual experiences or receiving special treats. You had no camera, but your memory of the experience is strong. Recall the most memorable moment of that experience as if it were a photograph. Then recall the events leading up to that moment, and finally the way that this special experience ended for you in your memory. This activity may require some time to reflect on to find the right memory to work with. It has to be a time and a place in their past for the person which provides them with benefits in the here and now.

A short drama from three living pictures

❋ This is a development from the previous activities, looking at ways of creating a piece of drama from the ideas that have come from group members about good social experiences, special occasions and strong visual memories.

Three moments in the remembered event are chosen - one near the beginning, one at the heart, and one towards the end. A living picture is made of each of these moments, as described in 'Bringing the photograph to life'. The group then creates the action that links these three Living Pictures together. How do you get from one moment to the next? There is much to discuss and consider. The critical factor is that the person whose memory it is has the ultimate authority on what to do throughout the whole process.

Exercise *Evaluating the drama activity*

> Obtain feedback from each participant on the process involved in this drama activity.
>
> - What did they enjoy? What did they find difficult or challenging?
> - To what extent did they achieve their objectives for taking part?
> - What evidence was there that the drama activity assisted their reminiscence process?
> - How involved did they feel in the drama process and the product? What support and assistance did you offer them that proved helpful to the task at hand?
> - What were their views on the final product?
> - Was the activity adequately resourced in terms of time, personnel and materials? What may have helped to achieve better outcomes?
> - What were your key learning points?

Reminiscence theatre production

This guide does not provide skills and guidance for producing a public performance of reminiscence theatre, although many of the above activities have been used in the devising process. That major undertaking will be the subject of a future publication.

By the end of Part 16 trainees are expected to have:

* acquired an understanding of how drama can be used to help people achieve positive outcomes from their reminiscences
* carried out and evaluated a selection of reminiscence activities using drama.

In Part 17

Next time we will be focusing on ideas for linking reminiscence to craft activities.

PART 17 Craft Activities

Introduction

> "The crafts make us feel rooted, give us a sense of belonging, and connect us with our history"
> Phyllis George

These may be craft activities that are well known to the participants and that they are still able to perform well. Alternatively, the activities may be completely new ones that people come to late in life and find that they can enjoy. There are many benefits to such activities, preserving old craft skills, passing on knowledge to others, recycling, reducing consumption, having fun, being creative, and saving money. In some cases the participants may not be able to perform the activity, but be able to act in the role of consultants and teachers for the activity organisers.

Needlework

There are many forms of needlework that your residents may be skilled in, for example, knitting, embroidery or crochet. The needlework activity can be used to create a conducive atmosphere for reminiscence chat on any relevant theme with the group. This kind of format is sometimes called 'Knit and Natter', and with some groups it can be the ideal group-bonding activity. Another type of needlework that emphasises the 'Make Do and Mend' theme is French knitting, which uses a large wooden cotton reel as the knitting spool, as commonly done by many people in the past.

Quilt making

This is a functional activity that became an art form and potentially a way of telling a story, using patches with different images in a sequence. The method developed across many cultures in response to the general need for bedspreads and clothing, but has also been used principally to produce decorative art such as wall hangings. Traditional methods can be employed alongside new technology that means photographic images can be added to the fabric. Text can be included with the images in the form of embroidered memories. The final work can represent important images from a single life or a number of people's experiences, and used as a trigger for reminiscence and storytelling. The emphasis could be on producing different tactile sensations that have comforting and pleasant feelings for people.

Homemade toys and games

This is a branch of 'Make do and mend' activity that is familiar to people of the older generation because it was how many of them, as children, used to have fun and play games. Expensive shop toys were not affordable. The idea is to use simple articles from around the house, things that would otherwise be thrown away, and natural objects to make playthings. This is something with which we are all familiar, exemplified by games such as 'Conkers'. All that was needed were some horse chestnuts, string and a skewer to make one of the most popular of all children's games and competitions. Part of the pleasure of the game is the whole process of collecting and preparing the 'Conkers'.

Articles from which toys and games can be made include newspaper, cardboard, stones, shoeboxes, string, play-dough and wood. Marbles can be made out of clay, with shoeboxes turned into targets for them. Mobile tanks can be made from cotton reels, using a match, candle wax and an elastic band. Dolls can be made out of dolly pegs with scraps of fabrics and pipe cleaners. Precise instructions for many of these toy-making ideas can be found on the internet, though don't forget that you may have the requisite skills and knowledge right there in your group.

Cooking

Cooking and food preparation is an excellent activity for reminiscence because of its all-round multi-sensory nature. Ideas could range from the simple making of tea to the more elaborate instructions needed for a main meal or a dessert. The art and craft of cooking lies in the ingredients, the preparation, and the arrangement of the food. From first collecting ideas for recipes through to the end product for tasting, all the senses are involved and the expert knowledge and skill of the group members are utilised throughout the process. Decisions about what to cook can be linked to seasons, festivals and special events.

Gardening

* If the group is interested in gardening activities, the garden or a conservatory may be the best place to do them ... they would provide exactly the right ambience for reminiscences related to the activity.

Raised flowerbeds and a work-surface would also be helpful for whatever gardening was being undertaken, whether it is planting, watering, weeding or cutting flowers.

As with all these craft ideas the expertise, skills and knowledge of the group members are an essential element of the process. For example, what should be planted at different times of the year, and how should it be planted and cared for? The group may want to grow vegetables and herbs, in which case the produce could be used in follow-up cooking activities. They may want to choose, pot and care for houseplants, or select cuttings of flowers to decorate the care home, thereby enriching the environment in which they live. Some of the group may also be skilled in flower arranging.

Working with salt dough or play dough

This is a traditional craft activity that can be used to make different types of things – figures, ornaments, 'pretend' food, decorations, marbles or abstract sculptures. There are different types of material that can be used for this purpose, including clay. The process is both creative and playful, with a lot of sensory stimulation through touch and muscle memory. Recipes for all these working materials can be found on the internet. You may want to bring the ready-made material to the group, or involve them in the making of it. Once shaped and sculpted, the salt dough models need to be left to air dry or baked until hard. The nice thing about this activity is that it naturally leads on to all manner of follow-up activities, such as painting the sculptures and putting them on display as hanging decorations or arranged on a canvas.

Making greetings cards

As with many of these craft activities, this combines a mixture of themes, making it all the more inclusive for group members. The making of greeting cards is a creative activity that touches on the different themes of play, special occasions, special people, gifts and 'Make do and mend'. Simple materials can be used, such as card-making paper, scissors, glue and coloured pens. Other flat materials can also be used, such as fabrics and dry flowers. The group can choose which events they want to focus on. All the major cultural celebrations and events in the calendar can be planned for, in addition to each individual person's special days, such as family and friends' birthdays and anniversaries.

Making decorations

Similar in nature to the above activity in the recognition of special occasions, this is a way in which group members can prepare the environment in which they live for a social and cultural event of some kind. The BBC Religion website has an interfaith calendar that is full of useful information about important days throughout the year for people of many different faiths. The group members can share their memories of how they used to prepare for these events, and how they used to make decorations for the home. There are also all the other cultural events and personal occasions on which parties are held. Whilst working together to make the decorations and party hats out of different types of coloured craft paper and paste, group members can share their memories of celebrations and parties of the past. Appropriate background music may assist the activity and prompt further reminiscence.

Making a memory box

This idea has been used to create museum exhibitions in many European countries. The aim is to create a small installation inside a box displaying an arrangement of objects, images and text that depict a person's life history, or some aspect of it. The original project made use of discarded ammunition boxes in order to produce something positive and creative from a symbol of destructiveness. Any kind of box can be used, the sturdier the better. The box is turned over and opened with the lid up, so that the interior of the box and the lid are revealed, and the space and surfaces arranged, decorated and filled in whatever way best represents what someone wants to say about their life.

* This is not something to be taken lightly, and requires considerable reflection about content and form. Generally, in such projects, the person has worked alongside an artist who has assisted them in making their ideas a reality.

Many of the reminiscence activities already described in this guide would help in identifying some of the significant objects, images, documents and texts from people's lives. How this is all arranged to make a visual statement about someone's life in a memory box is a great creative challenge, always resulting in a very personal and unique product.

Miscellaneous craft activities

The crafts and decorative arts offer us an enormous range of possible activities that can be combined with reminiscence. Other reminiscence craft activities that I have come across include basket making, hat making, woodwork, macramé, plate making, mosaics and rug making. You do not need to be an expert to offer these activities. The expertise may come from the group members. Your role is to be an enthusiastic novice who has good organisational and person-centred communication skills.

Exercise *Evaluating the craft activity*

Obtain feedback from each participant on the process involved in this craft activity.

- What did they enjoy? What did they find difficult or challenging?
- To what extent did they achieve their objectives for taking part?
- What evidence was there that the craft activity assisted their reminiscence process?
- How involved did they feel in the craft process and the product? What support and assistance did you offer them that proved helpful to the task at hand?
- What were their views on the final product?
- Was the activity adequately resourced in terms of time, personnel and materials? What may have helped to achieve better outcomes?
- What were your key learning points?

By the end of Part 17 trainees are expected to have:

- acquired an understanding of the use of craft activities to help people achieve positive outcomes from their reminiscences
- carried out and evaluated a selection of reminiscence activities using various craft activities.

In Part 18

We will begin to consider helpful approaches to working with people who have dementia.

SECTION 4 • REMINISCENCE IN DEMENTIA CARE • PARTS 18 – 21

PART 18 — The Person-Centred Approach to Dementia Care

Introduction

In Part 18 we will begin to consider helpful approaches to working with people who have dementia.

Many residents in care homes are either living with a type of dementia or may develop it as they get older. In a series of reminiscence projects we ran in London care homes 75% of the participants had dementia, many of them described as being in the advanced stages. They were still able to benefit from the reminiscence activities we provided which showed that:

* precious long-term memories could be accessed
* assets, strengths and skills could be appreciated
* feelings of security, self-respect and self-esteem could be fostered.

In parts 18–21 we will show how reminiscence activities can prove helpful to people who have dementia.

What is dementia?

Signs and symptoms of dementia include:

* memory loss – for example, forgetting the way home from the shops, or forgetting names and places
* mood changes and feelings of sadness, fear or anger or about what is happening
* a decline in the ability to talk, read and write
* in the later stages, problems carrying out everyday tasks, and increasing dependence on other people for this.

How the dementia progresses, and how the person experiences it, will vary from person to person.

Statistics show that as we get older a proportion of us will develop dementia, but that far more of our older population do not have it than do. The causes of dementia are unclear in most cases. The point is that dementia is not the inevitable result of living to an old age or living a particular kind of lifestyle. It could happen to anybody.

Exercise

Our understanding of and feelings about dementia

- Do a drawing that represents your different thoughts and feelings about dementia. You can include text as well. Think about what you know about the condition, different people you know who have had it, and the effect that it has had on you. If you can do this activity with a small group of interested people then it will generate a wide-ranging and helpful discussion looking at many aspects of the subject.

- After this discussion, write up four lists under the following headings:

  - Disabilities and weaknesses of people who have dementia – what they cannot do

  - Assets and strengths of people who have dementia – what they can do

  - Problems and difficulties of caring for people who have dementia

  - Successes in meeting the needs of people who have dementia

The resulting lists probably reveal a mixed bag of positive and negative experiences regarding people who have dementia and the care that they receive. Crucial factors in how people experience dementia are the quality of care that they receive and the quality of their social environment.

Person-centred care

A change in outlook and practice

> "To be effective carers we need to accept the 'reality' of the one we are looking after"
> Tom Kitwood and Kathleen Bredin

The way people are cared for, and generally regarded, will have an impact on how they cope with dementia. The Bradford Dementia Research Group has promoted a change of outlook regarding dementia care, with practical guidelines on how to help people living with dementia and their carers. A change of attitude is itself part of the solution to the challenge of dementia care. People who have dementia must first and foremost be viewed as individual persons who are experiencing, as they put it, 'failing mental powers' due to a disability caused by the dementia. With a positive attitude to what can still be done, an appreciation of remaining strengths and assets, and an approach to caring that 'puts oneself' in the shoes of the person who has dementia, then that person can be helped to feel secure, valued and kept in a state of well-being.

* The moral principle underlying person-centred care is that we, as health and social carers, need to make the extra journey to meet those living with dementia, because by the very nature of the condition it can be hard for them make the extra journey to meet us.

The old model of dementia care

Dementia is a devastating disease of the central nervous system, in which personality and identity are progressively destroyed.

The new model of dementia care

The different types of dementia are primarily forms of disability. How a person is affected will be influenced by the quality of their care and the quality of their social environment.

A challenge to 'stage theories of dementia'

It may be useful to have some understanding of whether a person is at the mild, moderate or severe stage of dementia, but this understanding needs to be combined with useful information about the individual.

* What are their strengths and assets?
* What are their likes and dislikes?
* With whom do they engage well?
* In which social situations do they relax and enjoy themselves?
* What are their lifelong interests and favoured activities?
* What can they still do with some support?
* Who and what are the people, places and times of life recalled by them?
* What are the best ways to trigger such memories for them?

In the absence of such individualised and practically helpful information, a stage-specific diagnosis is just another negative label. With this information applied to their care and their social environment, people can be well and content at any stage of dementia.

Understanding the experience of having dementia

Trying to put ourselves in the position of someone who has dementia can help us to appreciate their difficulties and think of ways in which they can be assisted. This can be done in a number of ways: reading written accounts by people who have dementia, observing their behaviour, listening attentively to what they say, and using your imagination to think and feel what it would be like for you if you were in similar circumstances.

Exercise *What would It be like?*

> • It would be helpful to do this exercise with a group of people in order to generate a range of views and experiences. What do you think you might be like if you had the signs and symptoms of dementia, and were living in a care home? What would you find frustrating in this condition and situation? What would you need? What would help you?

The needs of people with dementia

You already started to consider this when you were thinking about how having dementia would affect you. People with dementia have the same human needs as everyone else. To varying degrees from time to time they need comfort and intimacy, emotional bonds of attachment, a sense of belonging, occupation in chosen activities and a sense of identity. When these needs are consistently not being met, then they cause intense and distressing symptoms.

* The condition of dementia, coupled with an unsupportive social environment, can lead to a chronic deprivation of these vital human needs.

The invitation to take part

The way that people are invited to take part should respect and value their personhood and individuality from the outset. Gone are the days when people are taken into activities because it is presumed that it is good for them, or because it is 2pm, and they must be seen to be doing something.

There can be difficulties obtaining informed consent, particularly when one relies on words alone to explain the activity and obtain a person's consent. But we can help them to understand what it involves by showing them the process, exploring a range of memory triggers together, and enabling them to indicate their feelings, choices and preferences about the reminiscence activity. Are they showing a willing participation in the process? Are they happy to be there, and engaged in that process? Are they benefiting from the experience? These behaviours can be observed, and are evidence that the activity is meeting their individual needs.

By the end of Part 18 trainees are expected to have:

- acquired an understanding of the signs, symptoms and prevalence of dementia
- carried out an exercise that explores their thoughts and feelings about dementia, and their experiences of people who have dementia
- acquired an understanding of the principles underlying Person-Centred Care and the New Model of Dementia Care
- carried out an exercise exploring what it might be like to have dementia, and how one's needs would be affected.

In Part 19

Reminiscence activities have a part to play in enhancing person-centred care and enriching the social and creative lives of people who have dementia. Throughout this guide, it has been shown how reminiscence can meet important social and personal needs for people. Part 19 will look at how reminiscence activities can help people who have dementia.

PART 19 How Reminiscence Can Help

The role of reminiscence work in dementia care

> "Memory defines our individuality; it defines who we are; it makes us because it shapes our autobiography"
> Stephen Rose

✸ The principles of good practice in reminiscence work describe a person-centred approach to prompting memories, devising activities and valuing people.

With empathy and an appreciation of life history, reminiscence activities can help to maintain a sense of personhood and a social world for people living with dementia. Their ability to make positive contributions are recognised, and the reminiscence workers acknowledge that they themselves benefit from the relationship. Reminiscence work reinforces that people with dementia are human beings and unique individuals first and foremost.

Family and friends have a vital role to play in helping to provide personal background information that the person with dementia may no longer be able to provide, for example, knowledge about their hobbies and interests, their favourite pastimes and subjects of conversation, and their preferred types of activities. They will also be able to assist with matters regarding permission to record memories or use photographs of activities, when the person cannot give their own informed consent.

At present there are drugs that can slow down memory loss and relieve some of the signs and symptoms of dementia. Reminiscence work is a non-pharmacological approach to dementia care that has helped to relieve symptoms by finding enjoyable and purposeful activities for people. The effects of drug treatments may be enhanced if tied in with structured activities programmes. As well as the general benefits of reminiscence activities, there are positive outcomes that are specific to dementia care.

Helping to maintain personhood

Tom Kitwood described interactions occurring during reminiscence activities that can enhance the personhood, social status and quality of life of people with dementia. These are:

- Recognition as a unique person – through their individual stories
- Negotiation – giving the person real choices about how to take part
- Collaboration – working together with the person in a joint enterprise in which they are enabled to make personal decisions
- Play – opportunities for spontaneity, self-expression, fun
- Timalation (a word created by Kitwood) – taking part in activities that focus on the senses without the need for intellectual understanding
- Celebration – finding joy in the simple things in life
- Relaxation – with a calm and soothing memory trigger
- Validation – support and understanding for emotions expressed
- Holding – support for expression of painful memories and feelings
- Facilitation – enabling people to do what they want to do
- Creativity – the chance to contribute something creative
- Giving – showing interest, concern and appreciation.

This list is interestingly similar to the principles of good practice in reminiscence work.

Cognitive stimulation

Reminiscence activities can work as a form of cognitive stimulation and rehabilitation for people coping with dementia. There are many links with Cognitive Stimulation Therapy, an approach that offers a range of activities to engage group members, such as physical games, quizzes, food, exploring objects and creative activities. This approach is at the core of the SHIELD programme to improve cognition and quality of life for people who have dementia by involving them in life-enhancing activities. Reminiscence work focuses on the potential of retained memories for enabling people to engage in stimulating activities. Reminiscence is a means to a desirable end – the beneficial activities that it prompts and inspires.

Retrieving and making positive uses of long-term memories

- Through the imaginative use of multi-sensory 'memory triggers', reminiscence work is effective in helping people to access long-term memories.

These triggers work like props for people with dementia, supporting their memories, and if reminiscent for the person, can result in moments of clarity and vivid recall. They increase the chance that people will recognise something they know. And, as we find out more useful information about them, so we can learn how to give them helpful cues in the future.

A non-prescriptive approach to themes and activities

Choices about themes and activities are identified with the people taking part, and not imposed on them in a standardised way. The beginning of the project is the time for getting to know participants, and starting to identify with them their preferred ways of taking part. This creates a safe and stimulating series of activities that meets people's individual needs.

The use of reminiscence as an assessment tool

Reminiscence groups can provide useful information regarding people's recent memory, long-term memory and remaining abilities and assets. The primary aim of the group remains to engage with people in social and creative activities, but there is also the opportunity to gain valuable information that can help to enhance person-centred care, and assess needs. The relaxed and pleasant social context is more likely to find people functioning at their best and feeling confident about themselves, and so able to share and contribute more. In this way we can get a more complete picture of the person, including their personality and strengths, and not just evidence of cognitive damage.

Understanding behaviour and meeting needs

Some people with dementia are perceived as a nuisance or even a threat because of behaviour such as making and unmaking beds, wandering, and anger and aggression. Through reminiscence work you can understand some of the behaviour that might otherwise be interpreted in mistaken, negative ways: unmaking beds may be a remnant of parental behaviour or housework; wandering may be maintaining a healthy habit of going for an afternoon walk; anger may be a response to a fear of something caused by a traumatic experience, for example, a fear of uniforms caused by being a prisoner of war. Knowledge of a person's life-historical background can help us to understand their behaviour and find solutions to their unmet needs. Similarly, we can identify reminiscence activities for the person that can help them to feel useful and valued. All of this has a big part to play in person-centred care planning.

Exercise   *Your lifestyle and lifetime habits*

- List some of your daily routines and leisure activities, and consider how it would affect you if these were suddenly denied or taken away from you.
- List some of your dislikes and the things that make you feel uncomfortable or uneasy. How would you feel if these became a regular experience for you?

Opportunities for spontaneous play and creativity

There are no wrong answers in reminiscence groups, and there are many spontaneous ways in which people can enjoy themselves and be valued by others around them. The multi-sensory objects trigger implicit memories for people, and enable them to become the experts in the room, sometimes being the only ones who know how the objects work.

Sometimes, the objects trigger symbolic associations, with people using metaphor and analogy to represent experience. For example, a basket can become a sun hat. Such playfulness and creativity are actively encouraged as being part of the joy of life.

Protection against traumatic memories

Reminiscence work has evolved in response to the concern that people with dementia may be unable to defend themselves from traumatic memories. The effects of the reminiscence on the well-being of the individual are the primary concern. Sometimes people choose to remember and share sad memories that are about loss and hardship.

There must be a space in the reminiscence group for the sad aspects of life. Our role is to listen, understand and support, showing the person that they are safe and in control in present time. We are not responsible for people's bad experiences in the past, but we are responsible for how we treat the person in the present. It is about working with the person as an individual and trying to find out what is best for them.

When we are emphasising choice and control for participants, and using a stimulating and flexible approach, instances of sudden high levels of distress amongst participants in reminiscence projects are a rare occurrence. The norm is for participants to be assisted to recall positive experiences that improve their mood. These can act as effective distractions from traumatic memories, taking people to places in the past and activities in the present where they would much rather be.

Life story work

Individual reminiscence work

All of the activities described so far could be used in one-to-one work with people with dementia. It is a question of finding the most comfortable social grouping for the person, as well as the right kind of activity. One-to-one work affords the possibility of giving someone more time to express themselves if they so wish. It may also provide the opportunity to express emotions that are inhibited in a larger group.

An example of a one-to-one project for producing a Life Story Book is highlighted in Part 13. The final product must be engaging for the person, and work well as a memory trigger for them. It can be a book of memories, mixed with opinions, interests, likes and dislikes. Explore the creative possibilities that will produce a book that is a communication device for that person.

Similar information can be used to create Life History Profiles, made available to care staff, to help them appreciate the person they are caring for as a unique individual. Such personalised profiles and Life Story Books are particularly helpful when people are forgetting progressively more due to dementia. The person's permission to share the information for these reasons must be obtained, or, if there is difficulty in obtaining informed consent, then the permission of the person who represents their interests should be asked.

By the end of Part 19 trainees are expected to have:

* acquired an understanding of how reminiscence activities can help to maintain the personhood of people who have dementia, provide cognitive stimulation and access long-term memories

❋ carried out and recorded the learning from an exercise exploring their lifestyle and lifetime habits, and the effects of sudden changes in these

❋ acquired an understanding of the use of reminiscence as an assessment tool, and the relationship between life-historical background and behaviour

❋ acquired an understanding of the use of reminiscence to find positive activities and memories that can protect people who have dementia against traumatic memories.

In Part 20

In Part 20 we will look at some of the sensory and non-verbal group activities that have proved helpful for people who are coping with the signs and symptoms of dementia.

PART 20 Group Activities Focusing on the Senses

Stimulation of the six senses in reminiscence

As with all reminiscence work, the aim is to identify and play to people's strengths, assets and interests. The multi-sensory approach has proven particularly important when working with people who have reduced language skills and memory loss. The aim is to engage with them through sensory, non-verbal and environmental stimuli, as well as through verbal triggers that are still effective. Some of these activities focus on the senses, whilst others focus on performance and action.

Memory Triggers are of two main types – verbal and non-verbal. The general rule of thumb is that as dementia progresses, so it becomes more essential to employ non-verbal triggers and non-verbal communication. Normal everyday conversation, dialogue and questioning could come to mean less and less, and continually trying to return to it may only cause misunderstandings, pointless arguments and frustration. Having said that, a fully multi-sensory approach is best for whomever you may be working with because of the many choices it offers to people regarding what to remember and what to share.

There is no point in becoming fixated on any particular sense. We need to appreciate all the ways in which people can be engaged, and give them the opportunity to be so. There is no one rule that is right for all.

Exercises

Sensory activities

- Try doing the following exercises. Their meditative approach will help you appreciate how relaxing sensory activities can be, while at the same time sharpening the senses. After each exercise write down your thoughts and feelings about the experience – the process and the outcomes.

1) Close your eyes and touch and feel all the fabrics and surface areas within your reach.

2) Pick up a raisin and look at it in the palm of your hand. What does it feel like in your fingers? Squeeze it softly. What does it smell like? Put the raisin on your tongue. What does it taste like? Bite into it. What does it taste and feel like now? Finish chewing and eating the raisin.

> 3) Close your eyes, and in silence, listen attentively to all the sounds that can be heard, not just outside the room but within it as well, including sounds from you (breathing, digestion, your clothing as you move).

The need for sensory stimulation

❋ It is particularly important to have interactions with the sensory world when cognitive impairment is severe. In the absence of stimulation in the social and physical environment, people will seek out stimulation where they can.

What may seem like obsessive repetitive actions are actually a sign of under-stimulation and the person is simply seeking out the stimulation that we all need.

Reminiscence activities that gently stimulate the senses can give simple pleasures to people with dementia, and help them to feel at ease.

Making preparations

❋ We want the overall effect to be informal and relaxed, yet stimulating and engaging. This requires careful and sensitive selection of sensory stimuli, arrangement of the room, and choice of activities. Too much unselected stimulation can be distracting or overwhelming.

A multi-sensory and versatile approach will enable individual preferences and needs to be met. Focusing on only one sense or stimulus is wasteful of the variety of stimuli and interactions available. When doing reminiscence activities, artists/workers need to develop a broad eclectic approach, utilising all the arts and means of communication, and not seeking to raise their own art form above another.

This is what a mixed group of individuals with dementia needs. It may be that painting or clay modelling becomes the activity of choice for an individual, but this should not be the only choice from the outset.

Taking time to get to know the group members as individuals is the key task during the early stages. It is helpful to have some background information and knowledge about their special needs, but one of the aims of the work is to find out more about the individual, rather than make assumptions about what they can and cannot do, and do or do not like.

Preparing the space

The ambience of the room and its associations will play a big part in how people feel about being there. Every room has its own non-verbal atmosphere, mood and meaning for people. This is partly due to its design and partly due to how the room is commonly used. We need a safe and comfortable space, conducive to informal and sociable communication, and adjustable enough for appropriate seating to be arranged, and activities to be set up.

Some Reminiscence Rooms are designed like a time-capsule, as though time had suddenly stopped still in a time and place of the room-designer's choice. This can feel strange and unnatural, and limiting of what can be done in the room. It is better to include features that represent different time-periods, some old and some new, and different backgrounds to match the diversity of your residents.

Group size and selection

- It is better to work with a smaller, successful group than to have a larger group where people may feel inhibited and uninvolved.

The key issues are whether people can communicate as they wish within the group, and whether they are relaxed in that group setting. For group members to receive the support and stimulation they need to be fully involved, the ratio of workers to group members may need to be 1:2. It is important to have two co-workers with different roles at different stages of the session – one running an activity, the other assisting and monitoring the group members.

Mixed groups of people thought to be at different stages of dementia, or diagnosed with or without dementia, are workable. People can work together, understand each other's strengths and weaknesses, and see each other in a new light. They can participate in and enjoy the session in different ways – some more actively verbally reminiscing, some more passively appreciating and taking part in a non-verbal way.

Different types of memory

There are many different types of memory, using all the senses. They can work independently of one another. You can have a good memory for faces and a poor memory for names. People tend to have natural or learned preferences and strengths. The senses tend to work better when combined, which is why the multi-sensory reminiscence collection can be so effective.

There is a tendency to over-generalize about the poor memories of people who have dementia, for example, 'they've got no memory'. This is done with little appreciation of all the different types of memory and different ways of having memories triggered. It is also wrong to presume that someone is incapable of remembering something because they can no longer express it verbally.

Exercise — *Types of sensory memories*

To appreciate all the different things that people may be good or poor at remembering, look at the following lists of different things that are remembered through the senses, and tick which ones are your strongest.

- Sight – colours, film, photographs, paintings, objects, faces
- Sound – spoken names, sounds of nature, poems, music, voices
- Touch – fabrics, animals, tools, toys, natural objects
- Taste – different types of food and drink, remedies
- Smell – perfumes, herbs, soaps, polishes, tobacco, flowers
- Movement – dance, exercise, housework, games, gestures, skills, rituals

The list could be added to with more detailed examples. It is interesting to note how much of what we remember is of a non-verbal nature, and related to the senses and non-verbal activities – doing rather than talking.

Methods of evaluation

> "Those who cannot use verbal means to articulate their feelings and wishes will invariably find non-verbal ways to do so"
> Tessa Perrin

As well as collecting verbal feedback from participants, co-workers, care staff and management, family and friends, we can look for non-verbal signs as to whether or not your residents are benefiting. Some of your residents may find it hard to give verbal feedback or even consciously recall the activities that they have taken part in.

Tom Kitwood** provided a framework for observing non-verbal outcomes that show if people are benefiting. He called these Indicators of Well-Being. They are not reliant on verbal abilities, memory or logical thinking, but they tell us about a person's sense of security and contentment, and how they are feeling about the activities they take part in. These indicators are:

- Being able to assert oneself
- Being able to express a range of emotions
- Initiating contact with others
- Being affectionate
- Being sensitive to the needs of others
- Having self-respect
- Accepting other people around you
- Enjoying humour
- Self-expression and creativity
- Showing pleasure
- Being able to relax
- Helpfulness.

** Tom Kitwood: *Dementia Reconsidered: The Person Comes First*, Open University 1997

If photography or audio-visual recordings are made of the activities (with the necessary permission obtained), then these will provide the concrete evidence of the benefits achieved.

- It is also sometimes possible to obtain unexpected verbal feedback, especially when someone has been energised by a stimulating activity. Asking simple questions such as, "How was that? What did you like about it? What was that like?"

- In this way I have received comments such as, "It was like going back home,' "It was warm and cosy" and 'It was like being there all over again'.

By the end of Part 20 trainees are expected to have:

- carried out and recorded the experiences of various meditative exercises that focus on individual senses

- acquired an understanding of the importance of sensory stimulation, and the need to be aware of this in preparing for and planning activities: the use of memory triggers, the space in which the work is being done, and the group size

- carried out an exercise that explores different types of sensory memories, and listed those memories that are considered strongest for participants

- acquired an understanding of a framework for observing non-verbal outcomes that indicate whether or not participants in activities are benefiting.

In Part 21

In Part 21 we will look at some more activities that focus on sensory experiences, linked to emotional and non-verbalised memories.

PART 21 *More Sensory Activities*

Introduction

> "People who have dementia can experience the entire range of feelings. Dementia is no bar to emotional depth"
> Oliver Sacks

The following activities focus on an enjoyable and engaging non-verbal process, and use reminiscence primarily in the sense of finding and using a reminiscent stimulus to prompt pleasant feelings in the present. Feelings of peace and enjoyment can be experienced, having been triggered by a sensory experience related to a memory. They also provide ways of helping people to show their preferences and to make choices. This may in turn prompt some verbalised reminiscences, due to the personal effectiveness of the trigger.

Rummaging through a sensory memory box

Exploring a multi-sensory memory box containing accessible objects representing many different themes provides a perfect mixture of sensory stimulation and choice of reminiscence.

Furthermore, it provides other opportunities for stimulation of all the senses so there are even more possibilities that people will find the most appealing sensory stimulation for themselves, thus increasing the likelihood that they will be enabled to locate the right memories.

Feeling fabric samples

A selection of different samples of fabric can be sewn onto a piece of cloth or an apron, and passed around the group for people to feel and appreciate the different textures. This is very much like choosing fabrics, an activity that may well have been practised when they were shopping for clothes or buying materials for clothes. Remember to include a good mixture, including chamois and other leathers, tweeds, and so on, so that if there are men in the group they don't feel overlooked. The idea again is to give choice and enable expression of preference. The emphasis is on enjoyment and making choices – not on prompting memories, although this may well be an outcome.

Hand or face massage

These activities provide the opportunity for a relaxing experience that may connect to memories of feeling safe, cared for and loved. They are of an intimate nature, and may feel uncomfortable for some.

Bubble wrap

This is an example of a sensory activity that many people, with or without dementia, would find both stimulating and relaxing, but would find hard to say why they enjoyed. There may or may not be a connection with a sensory memory, but if it is enjoyable and soothing, it needs no verbal explanation.

Working with clay or play dough

As described in Part 17, this is both creative and playful, with a lot of sensory stimulation through touch and muscle memory. It has connections with kneading dough, food preparation, sculpting things and generally getting your hands dirty. You have to be careful that the material is not mistaken for the edible variety. People can take a real pride in the sculptures they have made, going on to paint them and put them on display.

Smells and aromas

These sensory triggers prompt feelings and emotional memories, for example, rose, lavender, cinnamon, rosemary, mint, eucalyptus, pine, vanilla, parsley or sage. As well as food flavours and the natural world there are also smells related to work, home, fashion, people, travel, entertainment, health care and hygiene. You can use a variety of foods, flowers, herbs, fabrics, clothing, perfumes, soaps, cleaning and polishing materials. Again, if you have men in your group, add even more smells that can act as sensory triggers - shoe polish, engine oil and car polish for example. It is more helpful to have the original sensory object than to have a bottled reproduction, because then the sensory triggers are combined as in the person's experience. It is especially important not to make this feel like a test situation, because you may be working with people who are conscious about having memory deficits.

Listening to music

With some of our favourite music, the best activity is simply to sit back and enjoy it. Finding the authentic recording, or a faithful version of it, is important in this case. It will be enjoyed in the version experienced long ago.

Sweets and confectionery selection

Fill a tray with a selection of sweets and confectionery, including new brands with some classic brands, and invite the group to take their pick. This activity combines taste with touch and brightly coloured packaging. Difference sparks memory in this case: it may not be the same as the favourite sweet, but it nevertheless has prompted the memory of the favourite sweet by its difference. As with many of these sensory activities, you may find that some people are then prompted to express opinions, likes and choices. It may even lead to the sharing of specific memories and stories.

Looking at works of art

Once again, with art forms that are primarily visual, the best way to appreciate and enjoy them is simply to look at them, and enjoy the thoughts and feelings that they evoke. You could arrange a display of photographs, prints of paintings, needlework and ornaments for this activity.

Combined sensory activities

With many of these activities it is possible to combine movement with the primary sensory trigger, making the experience more stimulating and reminiscent. For example, polishing an ornament, moving to music, music making, music while you work, or a walk in the woods.

Multi-sensory reminiscence collections

❋ All of the above is made possible by your communication skills and your multi-sensory reminiscence collection.

If reminiscence work consists only of asking people questions, then none of the above will occur. The simple everyday objects that you are putting together may appear as so much rubbish to some people, but it is through these very human objects that the lives and aspirations of people can be found and appreciated.

Performance activities

There is an important sixth sense to go along with the traditional five of vision, hearing, touch, taste and smell. The vital sixth sense is the sense and control of one's own body movements. It is another distinct way of perceiving the physical world, interacting with it, having memories triggered, and most importantly expressing and re-enacting experiences from the past. For older people with dementia, and possibly with visual and hearing impairments as well, it may remain a strong sense, and so a vitally important means of remaining orientated to reality and in touch with the world.

Below are some examples of activities that focus on performance, movement and action rather than talking. They may be abilities and creative outlets that the person who has dementia can still perform and enjoy. Parts 13-17 of this guide give fuller descriptions of how to facilitate these different activities. They are:

- demonstrating the use of objects, e.g. how a camera works
- dancing
- exercising to music
- making music
- miming a job
- dressing up – wearing hats, scarves, gloves, accessories
- posing for the camera
- taking photographs
- acting a part
- pretending we are somewhere else
- playing games
- singing
- reciting
- reading aloud
- making sounds and impressions
- painting
- drawing
- making a collage
- craft activities
- food making
- work activities.

Exercise *Evaluating the activities*

- After running each of these activities, evaluate it and write a report according to the guidelines in Part 8. In addition to these general guidelines for evaluation, refer to the Indicators of Well-Being listed in Part 20.

- What non-verbal behaviours were being demonstrated during the activity?
- Use the Indicators of Well-Being as a checklist to help you identify specific non-verbal outcomes
- What were the indications that this was an activity that led to calmness and contentment, or anxiety and displeasure?
- What were the non-verbal signs of either benefits or detriment to the participants?
- How did behaviour during and after the activity compare with behaviour outside of the activity?
- Give opportunities for verbal feedback to add to your observations of non-verbal outcomes.

Conclusion

In this section we have concentrated our attention on reminiscence activities with people who have dementia. We have stressed the importance of using a multi-sensory approach as part of person-centred practice. Reminiscence activities that gently stimulate the senses offer simple pleasures to people who have dementia, and help them to enjoy the moment and feel more relaxed. This sense of well-being can last longer than the memory of the activity itself, thus often helping the individual to continue to be at ease with themselves and their surroundings for some time.

By the end of Part 21 trainees are expected to have:

* carried out and evaluated a selection of sensory and performance activities that use reminiscence primarily to prompt feelings of enjoyment and improved well being.

In Part 22

In the next and last section we will look at special applications of reminiscence work, beginning with how to combine reminiscence work with oral history – the recording of people's memories for historical purposes. This is a special kind of reminiscence work that may be appropriate for those of your residents who want their memories to be preserved or become part of the heritage.

SECTION 5 • SPECIAL APPLICATIONS OF REMINISCENCE WORK • PARTS 22 – 24

PART 22   Reminiscence and Oral History

* Oral history is the recording of people's memories on sound and video tape, for use in historical research and publications. It preserves people's remembered and recorded life-experiences for the future.

> "History is all around us, in our families and communities, in the living memories and experiences of older people"
> Oral History Society

Most of the reminiscence activities in this guide are not recorded, and are not intended for further publication outside the group. However, it may be that some of your residents would enjoy having one or two of their memories recorded for various reasons. Oral History is an additional opportunity in reminiscence work that your residents may appreciate.

Exercise   *Why record memories?*

* Think about your own memories. Are there any you would like to record on sound or video tape? This is more than simply talking to someone about them, or writing them down. This is recording and preserving your voice and your physical appearance for others to listen to and look at.
* Which of your memories would it be good to record in this way, and why?
* Ask your family and friends what they think about having their memories recorded.

Who and what is it for?

As you have probably discovered, there is a lot to consider before making this decision. Some people find the idea of being recorded quite threatening, whilst others take it as a compliment. Some would accept their voices being recorded, but would not want to be filmed. They have to have a positive reason to be recorded. Possible reasons might include:

* to provide first-hand evidence of an aspect of social history
* to increase our understanding of living history
* to enable people who have been hidden from history to be heard

- to put the record straight about a misunderstood subject
- to give students of history more than the written word to rely on
- to convey the emotions behind a life experience
- to express personality through voice, behaviour and appearance
- to leave behind a legacy for loved ones.

The memories the person wants to share will influence what they want to do with them and how widely they want them to be publicised, for example, for close family and friends, for use in museums only after 70 years have passed, or for uploading today onto the worldwide web.

The person being recorded must fully understand and agree with how the recording is going to be made and used, and which memories are going to be recorded, what form it is going to take, and who is going to be able to listen to and view it. This is where reminiscence work moves into the area of oral history, but the principles of good practice in reminiscence work still apply.

- It is a big piece of work to take on, requiring preparation, recording responsibilities, skilled interviewing, transcription, editing and a good final product.

Possible products and uses

The recording could be used in a variety of ways to meet the person's wishes, for example:

- a film for family, friends and care home staff and residents
- inclusion on a website of memories
- part of a museum exhibition as an audio-visual record or text
- stored in museum archives or the National Sound Archive, for educational purposes
- part of a teaching pack for local schools
- part of anthology of reminiscences
- part of a multi-sensory reminiscence collection.

Individual reminiscence interviews

If the person has extensive memories to share, or if the memories are of an emotional or intimate nature, then an individual recorded interview may be preferable.

The pre-interview

This is when you make sure that the person understands and agrees with the recording process and the uses of the recording, and you agree with them the memories that they want to record and your lines of questioning.

Find out if they have any photographs, objects or documents that they wish to refer to. From this, devise an individual interview schedule that will be your guide for the interview. This will indicate how long the interview needs to be for the person to say everything they want to say on the subject. This may vary from five minutes to 60 minutes, but it is important to have an agreed length of time. Select with the person a venue for the recording where they feel most comfortable and relaxed. It is also important that there should not be any background noise that can spoil the recording.

The guided interview

The guided interview is more structured than an everyday conversation, and less formal and structured than a standardised questionnaire. The aim is to create a relaxed atmosphere, in which the interviewee can be spontaneous within an agreed area of subject-matter.

Basic interview structure

- Open with some biographical questions (e.g. when born and where from).
- Develop the main areas of interest, and enrich with personal detail.
- Close with opportunities to review and add some last thoughts.
- Give your thanks, and ask for feedback.

Guidelines for interviewer

- Ask clear and single questions.
- Ask open-ended questions that enable the interviewee to expand on topics.
- Ask questions and give prompts that you know work for them.
- Ask for confirmation of your interpretation of statements, if not sure.
- Encourage the interviewee to have a free rein within the interview structure.
- Do not ask anything beyond the agreed lines of questioning.

✤ Establish a good rapport with the interviewee through active listening, genuine interest, understanding and respect for their choices.

Activity — *Doing an individual interview*

Find someone to do a recorded interview with. Identify with them a special interest of theirs to be interviewed about. Agree the interview schedule with them and ask for their consent for the recording. Conduct the interview (about 10-15 minutes, giving time for closing thoughts and thanks).

Exercise — *Evaluating the interview*

Obtain feedback from the interviewee about how the interview went.

- Were they helped to say what they wanted to say on the chosen subject?
- How did they feel during the interview?

This exercise will help you to understand the parameters of your interview, in regard to content and timing, as well as gaining constructive feedback on your interviewing style, and comments that will be helpful when conducting your oral history interview with a resident.

Recording reminiscence groups

This can be sometimes difficult because of the tendency for people to speak over each other, especially when they are enjoying themselves. However, when you have a group of four to six people sharing memories on the same topic, it can be a very effective way of triggering lots of diverse experiences and exploring a subject in great breadth. You need to remind group members that they are being recorded, and that they need to take turns to speak. Reassure them that you will make sure everyone has their turn. The session has to be more structured and chaired than an unrecorded reminiscence group.

Technical aspects of recording

✤ Recording techniques and equipment are in a state of rapid development. The quality of the recording you want to achieve depends on the use to which it is going to be put.

If the voice is to be heard by the public, then it has to be of the highest quality digital recording, using a mini-disc recorder. If the recording is intended to be transcribed to contribute to material for a historical publication, then a mini-cassette dictaphone could be used. We will not elaborate on all the things that can go wrong with recording equipment! In essence, get to know your equipment well before using it. It is very helpful if someone can look after the recording process, while you look after the person being recorded. Put the microphone as close to them as possible, and reduce your encouragement and interest to visual gestures. Any sounds you make, other than your questions, can spoil the recording.

Consent forms

Please note, without going into the complex workings of UK Copyright Law, it is an ethical as well as a legal requirement that you obtain written consent from a person if you intend to make copies of their recorded memories, stating how the recorded material is going to be used. The Oral History Society has examples of such consent forms and the wording that can be used.

Transcription and editing

It is unlikely that the final product will simply be a copy of the recording, since this rarely comes out as the finished article. It is good practice to transcribe everything that the person has said in the interview, because this is the raw material from which the refined product will emerge.

Transcribing an interview is a lengthy process, taking up to three hours for 30 minutes of recording. Once you have the complete transcription, then you and the person need to edit it together with the final product in mind. There may be some mistakes that need to be edited out or corrected for a written reproduction.

The person may decide that they want to take out some things that they said. You have to make sure that you are only going to make a copy of what you have permission from the person to use. This means that the consent form cannot be signed until the final product is agreed. You edit the piece together, but the person you are working with is the final authority on how they will be represented (barring illegality). Other considerations about editing include:

* The law of libel (edit out any libellous or discriminatory remarks)
* Being faithful to the sense, meaning and tone of the overall material (not taking remarks out of context)
* Clarity
* Coherence
* Relevance to the intended use of the recording.

Exercise — Planning the recorded interview

Before embarking on your oral-history recording with a resident, spend time thinking it through and making sure that you have covered all aspects of the work:

* What is your aim for this project, and what do you want to learn from it?
* Have you enlisted the support of your manager?
* Have you arranged the time and space for the recording?
* Have you obtained the necessary written consent?
* What is going to happen to the recording and the product?
* Are you fully familiar with the process of conducting individual reminiscence interviews?

Listing and answering these questions will not only help with your confidence, but also provide a clear plan for this activity.

Conclusion

To produce a recording of someone's memories that becomes part of the heritage is an important piece of work, with benefits to that person and also future generations. It is a serious undertaking, requiring commitment and a range of skills, but it may prove, for some residents, to be precisely the motivation they need in order to share their valuable life experiences.

By the end of Part 22 trainees are expected to have:

- acquired an understanding of when reminiscence work overlaps oral history, and the purposes of oral history
- carried out an exercise listing the positive reasons why memories might be recorded
- acquired an understanding of the process of conducting and recording an individual reminiscence interview
- carried out and evaluated a practice individual reminiscence interview
- acquired an understanding of the issues related to the technical aspects of the recording, consent forms, transcription and editing of the recorded material
- carried out an exercise ensuring that all aspects of the planned interview are prepared for.

In Part 23

Here we will look at some points to consider when doing reminiscence work with older people from ethnic minority communities.

PART 23 — *Reminiscence Work with Ethnic Minority Elders*

Introduction

Many of the projects I work on in London involve older people from different ethnic minority backgrounds. I have also had the privilege of doing whole projects focusing on particular ethnic minority communities. In this part I will share with you some of the factors that I observed to be critical to the success of these projects. The principles of good practice as outlined in Parts 3 – 5 still apply. These additional points reflect my experiences of projects with ethnic minority elders.

The role of the elder in society

With many of the communities there is an explicit respect for old age and the wisdom of older people – hence the term 'elder'. Many of these projects have begun with a discussion about what the role of elders in society should be. This becomes part of the planning for the project, seeking to reinstate an influential and respected role for elders that is seen to be threatened by cultural, economic or technological influences.

Exercise — *What is the role of older people in society?*

- We all need a positive role to play at every stage of our lives. For children, young adults and middle-aged adults, these roles seems to be fairly clear, but for older adults there often seems to be no clear role related to their old age.

- With a group of colleagues and friends have a discussion about what the positive roles of older people in our society might be. Make a list of your main points, and discuss how older people can be enabled to fulfil these positive roles.

Aims and objectives

> "We are all united by our shared humanity"

Whoever you are working with, you need to be open and clear about the aims and objectives of the reminiscence project. There will need to be mutual understanding and agreement as to why these activities are taking place. For example, it cannot be assumed that this is something that is obviously good for the participants because they are minority ethnic elders, and they would want to be included. The sharing of personal memories with someone who is not a friend or family member may be something quite new and strange for them. There may be some understandable concerns about how the personal information they share will be used. There may also be some wariness regarding their involvement being mainly sought for token reasons – the box-ticking that they may have experienced before. We have to find with them appropriate aims and objectives for taking part – reasons for participating that meet their needs, not ours. What will they be helped to achieve in return for their time, trust, commitment and precious memories?

For example, in a project in Stepney, London, with a group of Bengali elders, we discovered that they had shared their memories before, but nothing had resulted from it. We agreed with them that their memories would be recorded and added to the archives of the local history museum, as well as featured in an interactive exhibition for local schoolchildren.

In a project with Chinese elders in Soho, London, the emphasis was on building bridges between generations in the Chinese community, as a lack of understanding and mutual respect was a growing concern for the elders. In another project with Caribbean elders, the group's aim was to illustrate the distinct cultural differences between different Caribbean islands.

With some of the groups I worked with, there was a strong interest in using reminiscence to preserve cultural heritage and pass on cultural knowledge to younger generations. The final part of this guide will focus on bringing young and old people together through shared memories – that is, intergenerational reminiscence.

Exercise — *The benefits of reminiscence work with ethnic minority elders*

> - This is for you to consider with colleagues and friends. What would be good reasons for wanting to run reminiscence activities with ethnic minority elders? What would be the benefits? Include benefits for your care home and yourself. Make a list of the main points arising from your discussion. For example, you may want to learn more about different cultural backgrounds. When planning the work with the prospective group members you would need to ensure that your aims match up with theirs.

Appropriate themes

The main themes of reminiscence work are universal, and so are of general interest to people of all ages and cultural backgrounds. For example, Food and Drink, House and Home, Work, Play, Entertainment, Travel, Fashion, Health, Education, Special People, Special Occasions and Special Places. Cross-cultural comparisons and contrasts add to our appreciation of these areas of human endeavour and interest. There is no one theme that you can assume will be particularly appropriate for any one cultural group. You are working with groups of individuals first and foremost, and you must work with them to identify their themes of interest. Whatever they decide they want to focus on, it will represent a subject of general human interest, which we can relate to from our own cultural influences. This is especially apparent in groups of people from different cultural backgrounds, when reminiscence themes help to appreciate individual differences whilst at the same time reinforcing a shared humanity amongst group members.

Varying attitudes to the importance of living memory and individual memory

Cross-cultural differences in reminiscing is not a well-researched subject. We cannot assume that all people from all cultures will choose to share personal memories or even highly value their own individual life experiences. Some people may instead value and prefer to share collective or community memories, and memories of the lives of ancestors. This is an interesting difference that enriches our work.

Cultural norms about meetings

When setting up the project and doing the early planning, it is important to find out the group members' preferences regarding how the reminiscence group is going to meet. Sitting in a circle in a meeting-room or lounge may not be their cultural norm for such a social exchange. When working with a Sudanese group in Greenwich, London, we were told that the reminiscence sessions would best happen during mealtimes with the group members, so that the sharing of food and hospitality was part and parcel of their sharing of personal memories. A group of Bengali elders preferred to have separate male and female groups for reminiscence.

The link person's understanding of reminiscence work

If you are working with a group of elders from the same cultural background, it is very helpful to have a person from that community working alongside you as your co-worker. They may be new to the idea of reminiscence work, and you can share your knowledge and skills with them. Their background knowledge and awareness of cultural norms would be very helpful to the smooth running of the project, and the two of you would have a lot to learn from each other as you work together.

Translation facilities

The interpreter's key role

Translation is essential if the elders are not comfortable or confident about speaking English. If they have to share their memories in a language that is not their first choice, they are automatically being excluded from taking part fully. Your co-worker may be able to do this for you, or you may know someone who can do this well as a volunteer, someone who is learning about reminiscence work and gaining valuable experience in return. However it is obtained, interpretation is required, and you would need to ensure that the interpreter has the necessary interpersonal skills, and enthusiasm for this specialist work.

Suitable reminiscence resources

Part of the planning stage of the project is to discuss with link-people from the community what objects, images, sounds and documents would be culturally suitable memory triggers. In this way, Age Exchange has created special reminiscence collections for different cultural communities around London, for example, African and Caribbean, Bengali, Punjabi and Irish Reminiscence Boxes. We often start with a general British reminiscence collection, exploring all the themes related to the objects, and then look for versions of these objects that would be specific to that community. Some are everyday objects that are easily obtainable, and some have to be bought from specialist shops.

Knowledge and understanding about different ethnic communities

One of the reasons for doing these projects is to learn more about people from different cultural backgrounds, and to improve understanding and respect between different ethnic communities. False stereotypic views about people from various ethnic communities come from a lack of knowledge and experience of individuals from those communities. We must try to have an open mind and a desire to learn more when running these projects, avoiding making any assumptions that have no basis in experience.

Regional and individual differences

Every culture has its regional and local differences that add to its rich and complex character. These differences are important to people, and make up part of their identity. When focusing on cultural and ethnic background, it is also important to recognise that every person we work with is an individual - a unique person with their own inimitable identity. Our aim is to represent the diversity of human experience, not to generalise it.

Some examples of activities

At the start of projects it has proved useful to focus on names and forms of greetings as the opening topics. Names can be explored as in the 'What's in a name?' activity. Forms of greeting can be described and acted out. What are the appropriate forms of address and gesture for different people in one's life? This activity recognises and respects individuality and cultural norms, as well as starting to trigger cultural and personal memories. It is a learning process for the reminiscence worker, and an appropriate and enjoyable way of initiating the relationship.

As with all reminiscence work we need to work from the general to the more specific in identifying themes of interest and preferred activities. The choice of theme may be influenced by the time of the year as well as by cultural or personal interest. To illustrate the potential for variety, these are some examples of activities that have worked well with particular groups. It will be different with every group you work with.

A Christmas drama

This was based on the difference between Christmas as remembered in Jamaica and Christmas as experienced in London.

Tug of war

This was played out by Age Exchange Project Workers and a group of Bengali elders, for whom the games of their youth was a favourite subject.

Dancing

This was a favourite activity for a group of Punjabi female elders.

The Windrush

Many elders have chosen to share and document their memories of migration to the United Kingdom on The Windrush. Some have also taken part in schools workshops on the subject.

Courting

This was a very popular storytelling subject with a group of older Vietnamese men.

By the end of Part 23 trainees are expected to have:

- carried out an exercise discussing and listing the positive roles that older people can play in modern society
- carried out an exercise exploring possible aims and objectives for reminiscence projects with ethnic elders
- acquired an understanding of possible cultural differences regarding the suitability of reminiscence themes, the importance of individual and personal memories, the appropriateness of memory triggers, and ways of sharing memories
- acquired an understanding of the key roles of the link person with the community and the interpreter.

In Part 24

The guide concludes with a feature on intergenerational reminiscence work – where young and old come together to learn from the past and build for the future.

PART 24   *Intergenerational Reminiscence*

Introduction

We conclude the guide with an optimistic eye to the future by focusing on bringing young and old people together through reminiscence activities. This is an additional option to offer the elders – a development from the activities that you have done with them. For some people, this can be the major motive for taking part – their main reason to share and pass on their life experiences: to work with younger people and to have a positive influence on the future. Intergenerational projects can take many forms, and I will share some examples from Age Exchange. The key factor is that there are positive outcomes and outputs for older and younger people alike.

The relationship between generations

Being young and growing older is part of the cycle of life. In any society there will be a mix of young, middle-aged and older people. How we define these age-types varies from society to society, but there is not much argument that when you are under 18 you are a younger person, and when you are over 70 you are an older person, and proud to be so. Somewhere in the middle is the rest of us. The question is – what is or should be the relationship between these different generations? In families there is some understanding of parental and grandparental relationships (although lacking in many cases), but in modern society it is not clear how young and old people should or could relate to each other. Worse than this, they often have very negative attitudes to each other, based on false stereotypic ideas and narrow experiences of each other.

Exercise   *What can different generations offer each other?*

> Age Exchange's name comes from the idea that each age (or generation) has something positive to give and receive from the other ages (or generations). Focusing on the young and old generations, have a discussion amongst colleagues or friends about the relationships and positive exchanges that might exist between them. Make a list of the positive contributions they can make to each other.

Exercise — *Something an older person has taught you*

- With friends and colleagues think about some older people you have known in your life – they could be older friends, relatives, neighbours, teachers, tutors, mentors, work colleagues, volunteers or people you have cared for at work. In pairs, talk to your partner about something that the older person taught you that was helpful to you in some way. It could be a piece of advice, some useful knowledge or information, words of wisdom or a practical skill (such as gardening, cooking or needlework).

- Conclude by writing up your thoughts and discuss what you might like to pass on to others of another generation.

The benefits of intergenerational reminiscence

> "Working with young and old combines the wisdom of the past with hope for the future"

From the above exercises you have now developed some ideas about the potential benefits of doing intergenerational reminiscence work. You can also return to the ideas in the previous part about positive roles for older people in society. It is important to have aims and objectives for the younger and older participants. Make a list of your positive reasons for wanting to invite younger and older people to take part in reminiscence activities together.

Project structure

Once clear about your aims and objectives for doing intergenerational reminiscence activities, you need to plan the project you would like to do, and the project that you are capable of managing. You will need good contact with a school, college or younger persons' agency, such as a youth club or scout pack. You will need to ensure that you have a group of residents who want to share their memories with younger people.

You will also need to commit time to organising and coordinating the planning meetings, reminiscence sessions and intergenerational events. My advice is to build a good relationship with a local contact person for younger people, and to start your intergenerational work with small-scale manageable events. Before you start the project, it is important to have decided how many intergenerational meetings will take place, so that everybody involved is aware of this. It will also be necessary to share information about the project with other staff in the care home so that they can understand the initiative and support its aims.

Links with younger people's groups

The contact person for younger people must understand and support the rationale behind intergenerational reminiscence activities, and be able to see how the younger people can use the experience to achieve various learning goals. Teachers can set schoolchildren work that is based on what they have learned from the older people's memories, and that meets various national curriculum objectives. Scout leaders would need to see how the project would enable the younger people to earn their proficiency badges. Drama teachers would require that their students were collecting material in order to devise a piece of reminiscence-based theatre.

The link person should have the expertise to see how the reminiscences can be applied to educational outcomes. You need to feel confident that the younger people are purposefully engaged in this activity, and that they will have adequate supervision from their teachers or group leaders.

Preparing the younger people

The younger people need to be prepared for meeting the older people, so that their questions and activities will match the identified interests and abilities of your residents. This means keeping the link person informed as to the memories and contributions of your residents as they emerge from the reminiscence activities sessions. You and the link person can help the younger people to develop a positive and respectful attitude to your residents, and to use the right approach to them – the person-centred approach that you have developed through your work. You also need to check with the link person that the stories coming from the older people are appropriate for the ages of the younger people you are working with.

Preparing the older people

As with all reminiscence work, begin with general reminiscence sessions, working with memory triggers and looking for relevant themes and ideas for activities. As you get to know your residents' memories and styles of reminiscing better, you can identify with them which memories they would like to share with the younger people. This is the confidence-building stage, when you are helping them towards finding stories to tell. Then you can work with the younger people's link person to discuss the ways in which these stories can best be utilised and the intergenerational relationships best developed.

The first intergenerational meeting

When both generational groups have been properly prepared, the first meeting between them is often of great anticipation and excitement. The older people have their stories, the younger people want to find out more, and most importantly they want to meet and get to know each other. If they are thrown together without support and preparation, they may somehow muddle through, but this is unfair to them and too great a risk to take. Plan the event so that you know the exact numbers of people involved, the ratio of younger people to your residents, and the seating arrangements for all concerned. This will largely depend on the type of activity that you have planned for them.

Ideas for intergenerational activities

These are some examples of intergenerational reminiscence activities delivered by Age Exchange, that have worked successfully for both ends of the age spectrum.

Reminiscence roadshow

This is based on the TV programme 'The Antiques Roadshow'. Your residents have identified some reminiscence objects that they know well and that stimulate them to talk about how people used to live.

Local schoolchildren have been studying these objects, drawing them and finding out what they were. They bring the objects to the older people (the experts), who demonstrate how to use them, and talk about what part they played in their lives. This leads to thoughts about how times have changed, and how we now meet the same needs in different ways. The schoolchildren go back to class and write up what they have learned from the older people.

Childhood games

The two generations come together on a subject of interest to both of them – play and games. You will have identified with your residents a list of games that they remember playing when they were young. Some of these will be known to the younger people; some will be a mystery, and they will need to be taught how to play them. Some of these games may involve craft work and creativity, for example, home-made toys such as peg dolls, shoebox marble arcades and tin can stilts. The main activity is the young and old people playing games and having fun together, but also learning from each other. The older people will also be interested to learn about the games that the younger people enjoy playing.

Written life stories with classroom activities

This combines intergenerational reminiscence with oral history. Some of your residents may have recorded their reminiscences, and expressed a willingness for these to be made available for educational purposes. Schoolchildren or college students read the transcribed text, learning about aspects of social history vital to their studies, and then get the chance to meet and interview the people in the flesh, asking follow-up questions and expressing their appreciation.

The teachers and tutors will be able to relate your residents' memories to study subjects such as history, citizenship and the creative arts, and the younger people can explain to the older people how their life-stories are vital to their learning.

Final event and evaluation

It is good to have a final end-of-project intergenerational meeting, where the two sides can come together, share their experiences and give thanks to each other for the mutual benefits.

The younger people can present their reports to the older people about what they have learned in a warm and convivial social event. Soon after this you can have a meeting with your residents to review the project and collect feedback as to what they have gained from taking part.

You will also need a final review meeting with the younger people's link person to discuss what was achieved and lessons learned for the future. Hopefully, you will have forged lasting links with the younger people's agency, so that other schoolchildren and students will be able to take part in similar projects in the future.

Summary of good practice in intergenerational reminiscence work

* When a project is set up, it is essential that all the participants are clear about what the programme intends to achieve for the young and old people involved.
* All intergenerational initiatives require careful planning and coordination, involving all the different agencies that are to be engaged in the programme.
* In projects where the older and younger generations are brought directly together, preparation needs to be carried out with each generation separately.
* Preparation and information sharing is essential with other staff in the care home, so that they can understand the initiative and support its aims.
* Evaluation should involve getting feedback from all participants at every stage of the process and then in a review meeting after the project is complete.

By the end of Part 24 trainees are expected to have:

* carried out an exercise listing the positive contributions that different generations can make to each other
* carried out an exercise listing the positive things that older people can pass on to younger people

* written a set of aims and objectives for intergenerational reminiscence projects

* acquired an understanding of the role of the link person with the younger people, the importance of joint aims and objectives, and the need for adequate preparation of both older and younger groups

* acquired an understanding of principles of good practice in intergenerational work, and a knowledge of some examples of projects that have proved successful.

Conclusion

That concludes this guide to reminiscence activities. I hope that I have been able to put across to you my passion for this work, but most importantly I hope that the guide has helped you to bring more reminiscence activities into the lives of those of your residents who will benefit from them. The more activities you run with your residents, the more ideas for new activities you will discover, because alongside the memory triggers, and guides to good practice, the richest resource of all are the older people that you care for.

EXTRA   *Using* The Daily Sparkle *in Reminiscence Activities*

Introduction

There are a countless number of different types of reminiscence activities on offer, and there are many different ways of organising and delivering them. It may be a ten-minute chat over a cup of coffee, or it could form part of a structured and regular group reminiscence session. It could be an open and on-going group, or it could be a closed group that meets for a fixed number of sessions over a period of time. *The Reminiscence Activities Training Manual* is full of ideas for many different reminiscence activities that have been used with good effect in reminiscence projects. These activities could be run as single activities with an individual or they could be integrated into a group session alongside other activities forming part of a group session structure.

Whatever format you decide to use, you will need resources to help you to run your activities and make them accessible to your residents. This is where *The Daily Sparkle* comes into its own as a valuable resource and starting point for all manner of reminiscence activities.

The Daily and Weekly Sparkle Reminiscence Newspapers

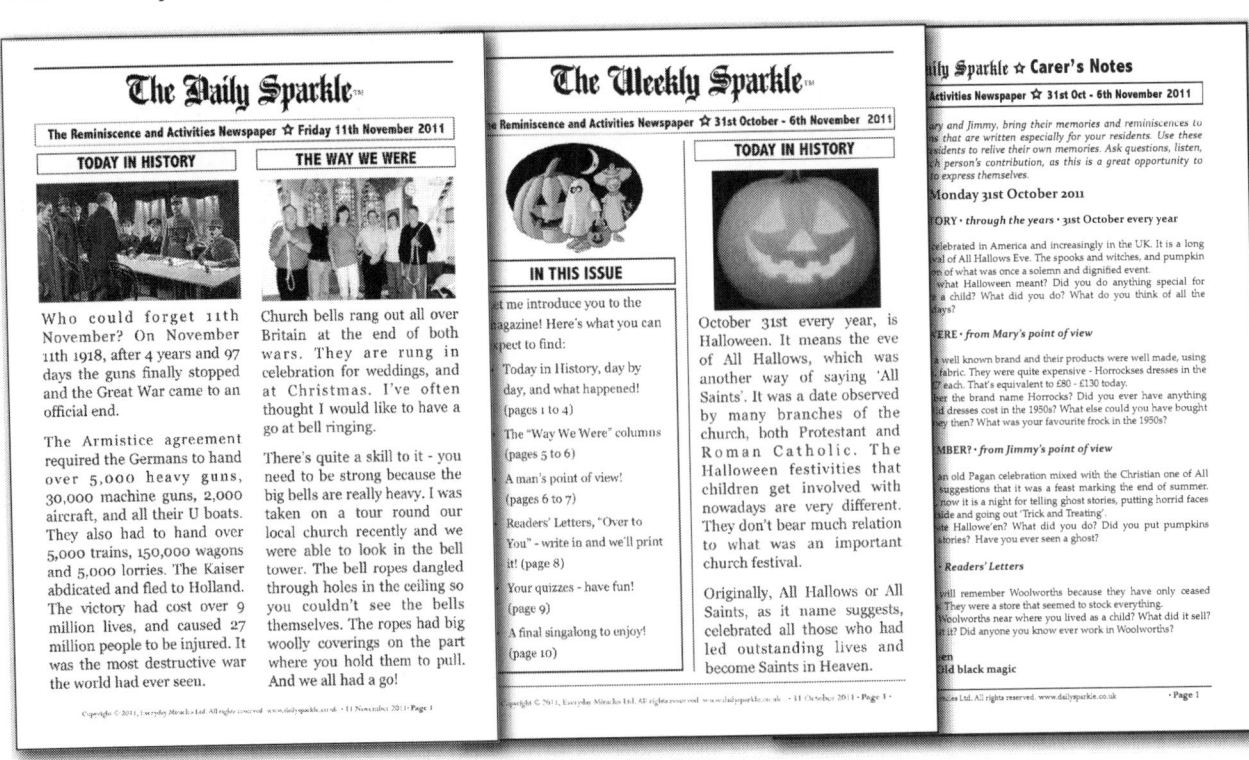

The Sparkle newspapers are a rich source of ideas and stimulation for activities programmes. The various features in each edition can help you to plan your session structure, get to know your group better, and inspire all kinds of social and creative activities. Its great strengths are its variety and its abundance of ideas, representing a diverse range of human interests, and so mirroring the diversity of people in care homes. With its daily provision of fresh thoughts and practical ideas, it helps to keep reminiscence activities new, contemporary and continually evolving: something interesting and enjoyable in the here and now, and something to look forward to.

As a source of ideas for your multi-sensory reminiscence collection

Each issue refers to several items that would be useful to obtain as memory triggers for your growing reminiscence collection. Some of these items are everyday objects that are all around us, but which have a hidden significance. The information in the edition explains what the item was used for: for example, a comb and paper to make a kazoo. Other reminiscent things are not old at all, but very much ripe and alive, such as fruit, vegetables and flowers from the garden. Some of the artefacts may take a bit of searching for, but can be found inexpensively in car boot sales, jumble sales, second hand shops and on Ebay; for example, Oxo tins, metal hair curling tongs and empty bottles of old remedies and lotions. *The Daily Sparkle* will continue to give you lots of ideas about what to get and how to find it.

As a source of information about twentieth century social history

The regular writers in *The Daily Sparkle* are rich sources of information about how life was lived in the twentieth century. They write vividly and engagingly about all aspects of life, sharing their personal recollections and prompting your residents to compare and contrast their own experiences. In fact they, and your residents, are the living authorities and experts on twentieth century social history, and by listening to them you will be learning about our heritage and our origins. This will broaden your horizons, and also equip you to better understand the lives of the people you care for.

As a source of ideas for reminiscence activities

In each issue of *The Daily Sparkle* you will find many ideas for reminiscence activities, suggested by the writers and based on their own memories. For example, in the issue of 31st March 2010 ideas for activities included the following:

- A collection of remembered nursery rhymes, poems and sayings
- A quiz based on the above
- A list of things that make you healthier
- Remembering the things that you wished for or wanted to be when you were younger
- A list of things that you don't see any more
- Home cooking
- Music making
- Singing and listening to music around the piano

These activities will help you to find out more about your residents and identify their interests, their most important memories and their preferred ways of expressing themselves. *The Daily Sparkle* gives you and your residents lots of options to choose from. It is important not to make assumptions about what will work best, but to find out from the residents themselves. It also helps to open the subjects out, so that the topics are not too narrow and excluding. For example, the piece about nursery rhymes focused on 'Oranges and Lemons', but you can enlarge upon this to include all nursery rhymes, poems, song lyrics, or sayings that your residents can recall. *The Daily Sparkle* can be a prompt and a starting-point for all sorts of interesting developments.

Activity – things that you don't see any more

The above issue of *The Daily Sparkle* brought up the subject of things that you don't see any more. This is a very large subject, involving all aspects of life. The piece in *The Daily Sparkle* uses Slab Toffee as the writer's example of something that you don't see any more. This was obviously important to him, and other now absent objects and things will be important to your group members. A quick search on the internet will provide you with many other examples of things that you don't see any more, and you can add these to Slab Toffee to give your group a starting point for their own contributions to what is a very interesting subject. You can help them with their thinking and remembering by breaking the broad subject down into its sub-topics, such as food, transport, work, education, health, games, shopping, housing and fashion. Use the piece in *The Daily Sparkle* as an introduction to the subject, then enlarge upon the subject with some other examples, and then start to explore and gather your residents' own ideas about things that you don't see any more, for better or worse! Could some of these things be brought back into people's lives, or are they best kept as memories? It may help to write this list of things up on a flip chart as a trigger and a focus for the group members. This subject naturally leads on to comparisons and contrasts between the past and the present. What things around us now do the things that the things we don't see used to do? A balanced overall view will arrive at the conclusion that some things are better now and some things not so good.

Exercise

- Following the activity, obtain feedback from each group member on their thoughts and feelings about it. Was it a good and interesting subject for them? Did they have the opportunity to say all they wanted to say on the subject?

- What emotions were prompted by this subject? Was it enjoyable to recall now invisible things, or was it tinged with some degree of sadness and loss? Were there examples from the group of things that you see now that are equally as good if not better than things that you don't see?

- What ideas came from the group regarding future activities? Would they like to find photos or do drawings of some of these things? Did they show particular interest in any of the sub-topics, such as food or fashion?

- Write up the list of the things that the group members don't see any more, attributing the contributions to the individuals who made them. This is a useful record of the work of the group and information about individuals in the group.

- Finally, what did you learn from the group about this subject? Keep a record of all the things that you are learning from your group members, and let them know as well. It can be part of their motivation for taking part.

As part of the opening to a group session

The Daily Sparkle can be a useful resource at every stage of the group session structure. It can help you to open the session, move the session forward and close it. Part of your task at the beginning of a session is to gently ease the group into considerations and thoughts about the past. The introduction to the daily newspaper strikes a topical note by drawing attention to something significant about the days' date, the significance being related to past events and news stories. This makes for a good way to bring the group naturally from the present to considerations and reminiscences of the past. It helps the group to come together by focusing on what's in the latest copy, and what's going to crop up today as a result of its leading article. Once people know and like *The Daily Sparkle*, it is also a very helpful way of bringing them together to meet for the group. '*The Daily Sparkle* has arrived. Let's see what it's got to say today.'

As a resource for activities throughout the session

As you get to know your group better, you will discover with them what kind of reminiscence activities they particularly enjoy – discussion and debate, writing, drawing and painting, dancing, singing and music-making, doing quizzes, physical activity, playing games, drama or doing various craft activities. *The Daily Sparkle* refers to many activities that your group will remember. This provides opportunities to repeat the activities, and not merely to talk about them. Collecting and collating these ideas from *The Daily Sparkle* will give you many different ideas for activities that meet the activity characteristics of your group. Combined with all the ideas in *The Reminiscence Activities Training Manual*, this will provide you with a rich resource to draw from and a wide repertoire of different activities to offer to meet people's different tastes.

As a way of closing a session

Part of the function of the closure of the session is to bring the group back to the present and move gently back into the swing of everyday life. Just as *The Daily Sparkle* can be used to start the group with thoughts of today's date, it can also be used to bring the group back to thoughts of today. By reviewing how the session began, what today's significance was and what activities took place in the group, you can satisfactorily close the group and integrate the session into the overall daily round of activities. Ideally you will have learned something new about the residents, and this may be incorporated into care planning and activities provision. The newspaper also always has an idea for a song for the group to work on, and this, or another song from a previous edition, could be a nice way to round the session off.

As a starting-point and stimulus for further ideas

It is important to view *The Daily Sparkle* as a stimulus for further activity, and not as the only activity that you will offer the residents. This would be to miss all the opportunities that such a stimulating publication will generate. Your residents will react to the reminiscences and ideas in each edition with ideas and reminiscences of their own. You need to be aware of this, and incorporate it in your future sessions. For example, there may be a reference to the playing of hopscotch in there. The subject for the group should not begin and end with memories of playing hopscotch, but should be expanded to include the playing of games at any time of the residents' lives. Hopscotch is but one example of many thousands of games that your residents may have enjoyed in their lives. To get maximum involvement and interest from your group, use hopscotch as a good starting-point for a wider discussion about games in general, with a view to finding out which games the group members might enjoy playing as an activity for the future.

Activity - the games that we play

This is an example of how a reference to a reminiscence topic in one activity can lead to a full-blown new activity. In the 30th March 2010 issue of *The Daily Sparkle* there was a quiz about games that involve throwing. Do the quiz with a group, and following on from this find out from the group if the games mentioned in the quiz were games played by them or of interest to them, not only the throwing games. Open it up to include any games of interest to group members. Games and play are big subjects, related to all times of life and all cultures. Talk to the group about the importance of play in people's lives. Find out from the group what games they played and what games they followed or were interested in. For example, they may not have played much football, but they may have supported a football club, and this is also a big subject in its own right. The subject should also include games they like to play or follow now, or would like to play or follow, given the opportunity. You can write up the list of games on a flip chart as a reference and a prompt for the group.

Exercise

- Collect feedback from each group member about this activity. Was the subject of interest to them? Did they enjoy the process of using the quiz as a starting point for thinking and talking about games in

> general? Was the quiz the most enjoyable part of the activity for them, and if so, would they like to do more?
>
> - Make a list of all the games that the group referred to, and make a note of games that were of particular importance to individuals in the group.
>
> - Was there enough interest in this subject to plan some more activities based on the theme of games and play? This activity was aimed at collecting information, and could be the basis of further activities that develop the theme. Games are better played than talked about, if people enjoy playing them.

As a prompt for activities and communication outside the group

As your group members take part in more sessions, you will discover more and more about their lives and their interests. In short, you will get to know them better. This will help you in all aspects of care provision and communication with them. You will understand better why they behave the way they do, how you can help them to feel better, how they like to be treated, and what kind of activities they enjoy outside of the group. Group sessions should not be the only occasions on which activity and communication occur, but should be regarded as helpful in revealing how people can be cared for and engaged with at all times of the day.

Conclusion

I recommend that you try to collect as many back issues of *The Daily Sparkle* as you can, because they are not just a resource for single use on the day of issue, but an archive of practical ideas for future use. Alongside the ideas from *The Reminiscence Activities Training Manual* and the ideas coming from your residents, they will help to ensure that your reminiscence sessions do not become stale, but grow and evolve to reflect the varied and remarkable lives of the people you care for.

Through subscribing to and using *The Daily Sparkle* to generate rewarding activities, you and your residents are part of a national and worldwide movement concerned with improving services for older people in care. You are actually putting into daily practice all the statements and intentions regarding person-centred care so often espoused by politicians and spokespeople, but so often neglected. You are part of a network of care homes and care workers that is raising the profile of older people and their carers.

Printed in Great Britain
by Amazon.co.uk, Ltd.,
Marston Gate.